RICHMON

Priests and Prophets

RICHMOND'S
Priests and Prophets

RACE, RELIGION, AND
SOCIAL CHANGE IN THE
CIVIL RIGHTS ERA

DOUGLAS E. THOMPSON

THE UNIVERSITY OF ALABAMA PRESS
Tuscaloosa

The University of Alabama Press
Tuscaloosa, Alabama 35487-0380
uapress.ua.edu

Hardcover edition published 2017.
Paperback edition published 2022.
eBook edition published 2017.

Typeface: Sabon

Cover design: Michele Myatt Quinn

Paperback ISBN: 978-0-8173-6054-2

A previous edition of this book has been cataloged by the Library of Congress.
ISBN: 978-0-8173-1917-5 (cloth)
E-ISBN: 978-0-8173-9079-2

To Kerri

CONTENTS

RICHMOND'S
Priests and Prophets

INTRODUCTION

Race, Religion, and Richmond

Arthur Ashe—Wimbledon champion, civil rights activist and Richmond native—created a stir in death as he had in life. Wishing to honor his memory, some Richmonders set out to erect a monument to the tennis great and humanitarian.[1] In spring 1995, the city's planning council approved a plan to place the statue on Monument Avenue, a vast stretch of road that spreads out west of downtown Richmond and is dotted with large monuments erected to Confederate icons like Robert E. Lee, Stonewall Jackson, and Jefferson Davis. The uproar that ensued from both black and white communities caused the city council to table the idea in order to carry out public hearings on the matter. In July of that year, the city council voted to add Ashe's likeness to Monument Avenue, but rather than face north or south (the indication of whether a general died in battle or not), Ashe's statue faces west with his back to the other statues, surrounded by children and looking to a future different from the past.[2] In the one hundred years between the creation of the road to honor the Confederacy, reinforcing white supremacy, and Ashe's death, Richmond's changing racial landscape—from the rise of the Jim Crow South and white supremacy to the civil rights movement—reveals the hopefulness of change and the reality of how far the city still had to go.

In the middle of the twentieth century, the civil rights movement agitated for a change in the oppressive system of legal and cultural racism. This book examines Richmond in the 1940s and 1950s to see how Christian leaders navigated the shifting legal and political battles around desegregating public schools. The discussion about desegregating schools in Richmond had a parallel effect on debates about desegregating churches and denominational institutions. Narrowing the focus to white Christian leaders in Richmond, we see that a variety of responses to the civil rights struggle developed within white congregations and denominations. The impulses toward change and those toward maintaining the status quo in race relations highlight a broad spectrum of both prophetic and priestly engagement with desegregation. Some ministers in Richmond called for a desegregated society. Often the conflict occurred within a denomination, including the bold move by Richmond Presbyterians to open their children's summer camp on a desegregated basis in its first year of operation, 1957, and First Presbyterian Church's open opposition to this decision. Sometimes, as in the case of the bishop of the Virginia Conference (Methodist), religious leaders led the charge to defend the segregated order. This tension over what a new revelation meant as it related to racial customs slowed the process of change and created an environment where no single, unified position developed on the question of desegregation. The fact that the conflict rested on practice and not doctrine, at least for some Christians, allowed individuals to interpret broadly what it meant to love one's neighbor.

The public challenge to Virginia's political leaders by Richmond ministers and the internecine debates between Richmond Methodists and Presbyterians reveal a complex set of reasons why white churches encouraged desegregation but also became visible examples of segregation. The development of black congregations as forms of institutional identity for African Americans from the end of the nineteenth century through the first half of the twentieth century *and* the growing sense that social change might include desegregation for white congregations are why eleven o'clock on Sunday morning continues to be the most segregated hour in America. The 1950s also demonstrate why that claim by civil rights activists carried such a potent rhetorical punch, even as black religious leaders never intended to integrate white congregations. In this way, this project explores the varied responses of white Christians to both the civil rights struggle and the attempt to keep schools segregated in the 1950s. It also serves a growing trend to revisit the period of the civil rights movement to examine white southern Christians.[3] Richmond, then, becomes a geographical space to evaluate the contested notion of white supremacy *within* particular congregations and denominations. The continuum of responses sheds light on Christian activism and its limitations.

A photograph taken shortly after the fall of Richmond to US forces in 1865 reveals numerous church spires in the city amid the destruction. Indeed, prior to the Civil War, Baptists, Catholics, Disciples, Episcopalians, Jews, Lutherans, Methodists, and Presbyterians had established a strong presence within the city.[4] This city of churches, as community boosters referred to Richmond, had held two convictions in tenuous balance: religion as a pervading ethos and slavery as a God-ordained institution. White religious leaders in the city defended the actions of the South during the American Civil War by giving religious credence to human bondage based on assumptions about racial categories. Though their attitudes may have varied toward the institution, all white Christian denominations agreed that subjugation of one group of people to another had biblical precedent. With Richmond in ruins, the Confederacy a memory, and slavery abolished, white Christians in Richmond had to construct a new order that made sense of the defeat in God's divine plan.[5] African American Christians understood the US victory in divine terms and set out creating institutions of their own. The distance forged between black and white Christians in the period after Reconstruction meant the twentieth century would see entrenched religious separation.

From the end of the Civil War until the middle decade of the twentieth century, white Richmonders, along with white people across the South, labored to reconfigure a society based on white supremacy. Without the institutional support of slavery, southern white citizens in general reasserted their political dominance over the region through the use of the single-party system and by constructing elaborate race codes.[6] This transformation took place in Virginia after the 1880s and mobilized white politicians by the turn of the twentieth century to work for the disenfranchisement of black voters with a severity not found in earlier race codes.[7]

Like the relationship between Christianity and slavery before the Civil War, the emerging New South rhetoric became intertwined with racial paternalism. Civic leaders in Richmond for the most part supported the goals of the New South prophets in the decades after Reconstruction—economic growth, industrialization, regional self-determination—and the city appeared ready to ascend from the ashes of defeat to its prewar prominence in the South. The industrial growth centered on tobacco and metal works, as well as the expanding retail and financial industries.[8] Richmond appeared poised to lead Virginia out of its provincial slumber; at least that was how white civic leaders understood their role. One historian has noted that Richmond in the 1890s was "the old city of the New South."[9] The acute sense of historical purpose that white Richmonders cultivated in their statues to Confederate heroes, particularly along Monument Avenue, also revealed Richmond's attachment to its past, and by extension, an ordered society with white leaders in control. Regardless of everything else, being white mattered in post–Civil War Richmond, and allegiance to conservative fiscal policy and notions of white racial superiority thwarted Richmond's phoenixlike ascent.

While white and black clergy in Richmond worked to ensure the promises of a New South—better sanitation, temperance, and improved race relations—the latter proved too difficult and revealed the limits of the New South's promise: construction of power based on race. The racial reality found expression in segregation laws separating black people from white people. The revised Virginia Constitution of 1902, which effectively disenfranchised black voters, assured white political control.[10] Industrialization, the mechanism that held out hope for the South's emergence from defeat and poverty, also reinforced separation of the races by connecting the modern category of race to economic and social suitability.

In many ways Richmond was an enigma. Richmond's boosters tried to position the city as a leader of both the state and the nation. Outside political forces, however, almost always dictated its life. As Democrats regained their stranglehold on Virginia, a succession of conservative leaders, culminating in Harry F. Byrd Sr. and his political machine, maneuvered to consolidate Virginia's racial politics. The rise and dominance of Byrd's political juggernaut over Virginia from the early 1920s through the 1960s revealed the complicated position in which Richmond and its leaders often found themselves. By the mid-1920s, the Byrd organization, headquartered in faraway western Virginia (Winchester) and aligned with Virginia's Southside (the region of Virginia south of the James River from Richmond to the Blue Ridge Mountains), dominated Virginia's political life.[11] Richmond's leadership with its fiscal conservative leanings followed Byrd's demand for economic frugality, but that loyalty wreaked havoc on Virginia's educational system when Byrd called for massive resistance to the US Supreme Court decision *Brown v. Board of Education* (which called for desegregation of public schools in the mid-1950s), and Richmond—in both its legislative and municipal sense—became a pawn in the struggle to keep schools segregated.

As Beth Schweiger and Samuel Shepherd have pointed out, the growth of evangelical witness in Richmond from the middle of the nineteenth century through the 1920s showed how white Baptists, Methodists, and Presbyterians grew in number but also social stature. Richmond's Catholics and Jews followed similar patterns during the same period though their overall numbers would be fewer than the Protestant denominations'. Episcopalians, long a fixture in Virginia life, maintained a certain status even when their numbers were fewer than white Baptists, Methodists, and Catholics. African American Baptists, however, outpaced all of these groups. To a lesser extent, Methodists, other Protestant bodies, and an important Catholic ethnic parish contributed to a significant African American Christian presence in the city. African American Christians' full story in Richmond has yet to be told, but their witness prompted calls by white religious leaders to create a more just society. The growth in the 1920s was followed by a brief contraction of the population of the city in the 1930s, which also affected congregations.

As an example of how strong cultural Christianity became in Richmond, the 1936 survey of religious bodies in the United States revealed the percentage of the total population of the city who participated in the largest denominations. Black Baptists had the largest number of churches in Richmond and the highest membership numbers. Black Baptists had almost double the number of congregations (43) as the next closest denomination, Methodist Episcopal Church, South, which had 23. Combined with Southern Baptists, there were over 41,000 Baptists in Richmond. In a city with over 193,000 people, collectively the largest denominational grouping (Baptists) made up more than twenty-one percent of the total population. There were just over 16,000 Southern Methodists in the city (a little over twelve percent). Catholics (at 12,000) and Protestant Episcopal Church members (at a little over 10,000) represented another thirteen percent. Black Catholics, Episcopalians, and Methodists enlarged the Christian population of the city. While the numbers attached to the survey are open to dispute, Richmond's Christian community had made significant progress in creating a cultural dominance. Once the population and economic boom hit in the aftermath of World War II, the continued growth within denominations in the 1950s highlighted a new level of respect and influence in the larger society for Christian ministers in the city.

As an example of the increase in Richmond's growth, the neighborhood of Barton Heights saw a rapid increase in church membership and attendance by the early 1950s. White churches "canvased" the area and located 7,542 residents. Of that number, 220 did not respond to the survey; 2,226 people indicated that their membership or their "preference" was Baptist, while Methodists numbered at 1,822 and 1,128 identified as Catholic. Presbyterians and Episcopalians round out the top five groups at over 750 each. Only eighty-two indicated no preference.[12] If the nineteenth and early twentieth centuries had seen Christians work hard to expand their dominance (as Schweiger and Shepherd note), the middle of the twentieth century showed the fruits of that labor. Evangelicals and Catholics had overcome suspicion from all sides to dominate the cultural landscape. While it might appear as a truism that Christianity held cultural dominance, religious engagement in political issues had often been seen as interference. By the early 1950s, it appeared that ministers could engage in public dialogue since their cultural clout had grown. Richmond's white ministers would be called on to help shape the future, but their position on desegregation put them in the crosshairs of segregationists.

The postwar boom in church attendance, however, had begun to put pressure on sanctuaries built thirty years earlier for congregations half the size of the ones gathering every Sunday of the early 1950s. By the mid-1950s, Barton Heights underwent a significant demographic shift as well. Within one decade the neighborhood went from almost entirely white residents to almost entirely black residents. Similar patterns occurred across the city. Chandler Middle School in Barton Heights became the first public school in Richmond to desegregate in 1960. The churches in this area, as well as across Richmond, had to engage the desegregation discussion because pupil placement occurred in neighborhood contexts, which also meant congregations were keenly aware of neighborhood change. White religious leaders in Richmond were fully aware of this issue and entered into the discussion, often pushing for desegregated churches as well. Even as congregational numbers grew and ministers' influence expanded, the social pressure to keep life segregated placed Richmond ministers on a collision course with forces in their own congregations as they challenged the governor of Virginia and the state legislature.

Richmond served as home to an intellectual defense of segregated public schools, particularly through the writing of the *Richmond News Leader* editor James J. Kilpatrick. Kilpatrick, a Catholic who stood in opposition to his bishop's position on desegregation, wrote forcefully from 1955 to 1959 on the editorial pages of the

Richmond News Leader for a resistance by all white citizens to any attempt by the courts or politicians to desegregate public schools. Mississippi's White Citizens Council reprinted his columns, and he corresponded with US Senators James O. Eastland and Harry F. Byrd on a regular basis. Richmond ministers, however, challenged Kilpatrick and the political leadership of Virginia. There are hints of a shift in religious leadership in Richmond to challenge the segregated order in the aftermath of the *Brown* decision in May 1954. Four religious editors located in Richmond sparred with Kilpatrick and others who attempted to resist the Supreme Court's ruling. The editors' responses also showed there would be no single voice for Christianity in the desegregation crisis. These skirmishes paled in comparison to the manifesto against massive resistance published by the Richmond Ministers' Association (RMA) in 1957. The RMA used space in the morning Richmond paper, the *Richmond Times-Dispatch*, to call into question the work of the governor, the state legislature, and by extension Kilpatrick's attempt to keep the debate focused on constitutional claims instead of white supremacy. The ministers' statement attempted to shame the governor and state legislators and announce the ministers' commitment to desegregation. The negative response by Kilpatrick and others revealed the troubled waters the ministers were willing to enter. The manifesto signaled a change by white clergy but that did not mean their congregants or society were willing to follow.

Massive resistance, a white political movement in the South to keep public schools segregated no matter the cost, revealed the lengths to which the political leadership in Virginia, as well as across the South, would go during the late 1950s. Richmond, however, failed to be a contested educational arena like Norfolk, Charlottesville, or Warren County, or especially the catastrophic example set by Prince Edward County. By 1958 when the first petition for desegregation was made in Richmond, groups of Richmonders had been working for more than four years to ready the city. Many of the leading figures in these organizations were white religious leaders, both lay and clergy, working in organizations outside of denominational structures. Meanwhile, the political forces advocating continued segregation used stalling tactics that allowed upwardly mobile white people to continue to migrate quietly into the counties just north and south of the city's borders, a strategy of "white flight" begun earlier in the decade.[13]

Richmond, therefore, weathered the massive resistance years without the national media publicizing their resistance or federal troops carrying out federal desegregation orders on national television. Since there were few "outside agitators," the debates were homegrown and suggested that religious leaders in Richmond saw this moment as a chance to move forward on racial issues. Examining their confrontation with the political order and their own denominational structures, we can see how Christianity's authority supported change and the status quo simultaneously. By 1960, college students from Virginia Union University along with seminarians from Union Theological Seminary in Richmond made sure the national media attention turned to Richmond when they boycotted downtown department stores. The moderate successes for desegregation in Richmond appeared too small and incremental when responses by civil rights activists became openly defiant, particularly in the early 1960s. The fact that white congregations became part of the spectacle of maintaining segregation suggests that little had changed regarding racial attitudes. Change was indeed underway. The citizens of Richmond engaged in an elaborate dialogue about desegregation and what it would mean to the city and its churches. The period from just before the *Brown* decision until students from Virginia Union University participated in region-wide sit-in protests in 1960 provides a rich landscape for understanding the complex and complicated religious responses to civil rights campaigns and segregationists' attempts to thwart that activity. The ministerial voices calling for desegregation were loud and often prophetic. Change, however, came slowly.

For most white Christians in Richmond, as well as the nation at large, during the 1940s and 1950s a segregated life was part of God's divine plan—in social settings and in churches. There were, however, white religious leaders like John H. Marion Jr. and Aubrey N. Brown Jr., both Presbyterians, pushing congregations to think more critically about how segregation violated God's will for humanity. There were other white religious leaders who called for change to be carried out in a deliberate and cautious way. White ministers like Clyde Hickerson worked closely with leaders at Virginia Union University to help white Baptists understand the needs of African Americans in the city but also oversaw the departure of Barton Heights Baptist Church from its home when members became uncomfortable with the arrival of black residents in the neighborhood. There were also ardent segregationists like Bishop Paul N. Garber in the Virginia Conference of the Methodist Church, even as some of his ministers were the most outspoken advocates of desegregation both in schools and churches. These disparate voices created competing claims for how white congregations should respond to the school desegregation and, more importantly, congregational desegregation. In the end, Garber's vision for the church, the norm in the early 1950s, disappeared with the successes of the civil rights movement. Marion's call for complete integration, however, also failed to materialize. After the chaotic days of black protests and white opposition in the 1960s, congregations were open to desegregation but remained segregated.

Priests, Prophets, and Revelation

Christianity has struggled almost from its inception with how to situate itself within social structures. By the 1950s in Richmond, it would have been hard to see how being a white Christian or a white Richmonder was somehow different. Any call to change would have been met with suspicion and rejection. Those ministers who advocate for a desegregated society worked against the grain. The desegregation struggle over public schools required religious leaders to think theologically about those events. The call for change, now seen as prophetic, was less clear in those days. The time between losing the hold of an old claim and the acceptance of a new one reveals a great deal about religious communities.

In Jewish and Christian traditions, these impulses take shape in the roles of priest and prophet. Prophets appear to push the religious community closer to the ideal, often calling the faithful back to a more distant or purer understanding of the tradition. This ideal serves a corrective purpose for the misreading, as understood by prophets, of the authoritative text. Priests, however, are necessary since they can guard against false prophets. In some cases, the priest is a prophet. Most of the church's history has occurred living between the need to ground the religion in a social setting and keep the same setting from suffocating the promise of God's presence. Religious communities are caught between those two impulses as they make their way forward in the "world." And the emphasis on individual revelation in the American context complicates our understanding even more. A new revelation then is rarely clear to everyone at the same time. The disconnect from the former way of seeing an issue in theological light comes slowly, if at all, and finds expression in something less than the ideal.

Flannery O'Connor helps us understand this process in her short story "Revelation." She places a small group of white characters in the confined space of a doctor's office waiting room to explore the relationship of piety, racial understanding, and progress. Few seats are available as a white couple, Mrs. Turpin and her husband, Claud, enter the room, creating a tension over propriety and, by extension, southern Christian racial assumptions. The collection of folks sitting range from what Mrs. Turpin defines as "white trash" to a classy woman, similar to herself. The presence of a black character spurs every conceivable white southerners' notions about African Americans at mid-century into open conversation after the deliveryman leaves. She tries to carry on polite conversation, but Mrs. Turpin's internal monologue, which is impolite in the southern way of saying nice things aloud but meaning them in negative ways, finally escapes and enters the room. "When I think who all I could have been besides myself and what all I got, a little of everything, and a good disposition besides, I just feel like shouting, 'Thank you, Jesus, for making everything the way it is! It could have been different!'"[14] Mrs. Turpin shapes her religious outlook to her social status.

Unaware of the internal monologue in another character, the

protagonist sits comfortable in her judgment. It is not until she feels the impact of a book hitting her forehead that Mrs. Turpin realizes there are consequences for her outward expressions. The classy woman's daughter, Mary Grace, threw her textbook—*Human Development*—in anger. In the space between the hand of the thrower and the target, the chasm between white southern Christians' notions of piety and race closed quickly. The violence of the thrown book startles Mrs. Turpin. Following the trajectory of the book, Mary Grace lunges at the older woman with both of them falling to the ground. Mrs. Turpin responds defensively, shocked at the manner of the confrontation. The moment, however, creates doubt, even as she spends the rest of the story convincing herself that she is not bound for hell, as Mary Grace suggested, for believing what she believes. O'Connor suggests that change came to Mrs. Turpin, but it came slowly and not completely, even in the final revelation.

After the scene in the doctor's office, Mrs. Turpin looks for consolation from her husband, Claud, the hired hands ("lazy colored workers," she calls them), and finally her hogs. In a moment of moral desperation, Mrs. Turpin cries out in a Job-like prayer of anger and frustration at the hogs. "'Go on,' she yelled, 'call me a hog! Call me a hog again. From hell. Call me a wart hog from hell. Put that bottom rail on top. There'll still be a top and bottom!'" O'Connor gives Mrs. Turpin one final exclamation before the vision, a call out to an indefinite source. "Who do you think you are?" As her eyes shift from the hogs to the horizon, she has a transcendent vision that shaped all of her inferiors—lower-class white people and all black people—headed into heaven ahead of her. The characters of the "vast horde of souls" were not fully transformed in Mrs. Turpin's revelation because they were "shouting and clapping and leaping like frogs." "And bringing up the end of the procession was a tribe of herself and Claud, who had always had a little of everything and the God-given wit to use it right. She leaned forward to observe them closer. They were marching behind the others with great dignity, accountable as they had always been for good order and good common sense and respectable behavior.

They alone were on key. Yet she could see by their shocked and altered faces that even their virtues were being burned away."

The story provides a metaphor for the decade of the 1950s regarding white southerners' responses to the shifting racial landscape and the direct challenges of the civil rights movement. White Christians struggled to make sense out of a world turning upside down. As good-hearted as white southerners might have thought themselves to be, the US Supreme Court ruling in *Brown* pressed the issue of desegregation in ways they were not ready to embrace. In fact, integrated public schools forced religious people to examine their sacred notions of segregated life, something white ministers in Richmond had already been suggesting. Just as Mrs. Turpin cried out for understanding as to why she—a good, Christian woman—had been targeted as corrupt, white southern Christians did not understand why their way of life was challenged. For some white Christians shock turned to revelation, as with Mrs. Turpin even if it was not always complete; for many others, however, it caused only a minor stir until they could reorganize the status quo to a new order.

This book examines Richmond, Virginia, during the late 1940s and the 1950s to understand how white Christians struggled with segregationist politicians and their own understanding of a segregated society.[15] In the process this political engagement created tensions within denominational bodies and congregations. Their failures and successes suggest that we have more to learn about how Christians navigated the challenges of the 1950s. In the same way that O'Connor frames the story as a struggle created by an external threat with the protagonist responding to the event, our understanding of southern white Christians follows a similar pattern. Only after confrontations by African Americans—in the form of legal challenges or direct action movements—did white southerners, particularly white Christians, begin to change their collective minds regarding racism in their institutions. Without those actions, white southerners as a whole would not have had to think more broadly about desegregation. There were, however, individuals in the South who pushed for change in Christian institutions long before the direct action campaigns, and their successes have not been noted because the form of change that came was slow and incomplete. In Richmond, at least, we find congregations and their ministers engaged in the political crisis of the day. The broad spectrum of responses reveals how prophetic voices bring about change even if it looked like nothing had happened.

I

THE GOSPEL WORKING OUT

"The happiest and most effective Christians," Rev. John H. Marion Jr. exhorted, "are those for whom, somewhere, Christianity has become a consuming love and a mastering passion."[1] The preacher at Grace Covenant Presbyterian Church, Richmond, had sojourned to Richmond from his native South Carolina by way of Charlotte, North Carolina, in the early 1940s and settled into a nearly two-decade ministry in local churches, as a denominational administrator, and as executive director of the Virginia Council on Human Relations (VCHR). The biblical text used for the sermon was Act of the Apostles (26:25), where a Roman official named Festus called Paul's behavior mad and Paul responded: "I am not mad, most noble Festus, but speak forth the words of truth and soberness." The sermon, preached during the early 1940s, used Lloyd Douglas's novel *Magnificent Obsession*, which by the time of the sermon had been turned into a successful Hollywood movie with Irene Dunne and Robert Taylor, to illustrate what Paul's response would be like in the twentieth century. Marion challenged his hearers to remember their loyalty to Christ above all other loyalties, including wealth and nation. Marion's use of both the novel and the biblical text revealed a southern minister willing to have the gospel work outward from personal piety to public engagement. In the context of this sermon, he did little to challenge his hearers beyond a typical Sunday morning sermon, but Marion left hints at his willingness to push against social norms, which he did for the remainder of his life.

Douglas's novel, published in 1929, centers on an ambitious young man setting out to make money and a name. His plans are interrupted when a stranger reveals that the secret to a happy life is to give everything—time, money, and talent—away. The secret was to do good works for others without their knowledge and allow those works to sustain the individual's spiritual life. Marion noted that the plan worked because the obsession "grips him, it fires him, it holds him, and, for the rest of his life, it animates and motivates all his actions." The young man developed "a magnificent obsession," one that the followers of Christ would do well to embrace. Given that Douglas's ministerial training and career as a pastor found expression in his novels, Marion's use of *Magnificent Obsession* to explain St. Paul's response to Festus revealed how in the second quarter of the twentieth century ministers were attempting to find a way forward for a social Christianity in the currents of American life and in southern forms of Christian practice. In a world at war and reliant on the consumption of things, Marion's call to a Christ-centered life that shunned reliance on war or money would have appeared odd.

The single line Marion emphasized from Acts comes after Festus claimed that the followers of Jesus were mad to believe that a person once dead was alive. Paul and early believers were struggling with religious movements within Judaism over how to interpret Jesus within God's plan. For the early church, their assertion that Jesus had risen from the dead and ascended to God ran counter to the belief system of those in control of the Temple and Jewish governing structure in Jerusalem, leaving the Romans to sort out whose interpretation was the least harmful approach to their empire. From the outside, Paul's logic about Jesus's resurrection appeared crazy to some Jewish leaders and almost all Romans. For those who agreed with Paul, his understanding of Jesus made perfect sense. *Within* the larger church, however, tensions arose over what following Jesus meant. As became clear in Acts and Paul's letters, Jesus's ministry meant different things to different groups. For more than two millennia the church has struggled with others and itself to make sense of what it meant to be a disciple of Jesus. In the twentieth century South those competing visions found expression in the question of racial segregation.

From the 1940s through the 1960s, there were many white preachers in the American South who worked to bring about a desegregated kingdom of God on earth. When ministers like John Marion talked about an obsession that resembled an all-consuming love of Jesus, they framed that love in terms of a desegregated society, including churches.[2] Emphasizing a gospel that challenged southern norms, these preachers found themselves at risk in the larger community but also in their congregations. Every pastor struggles in that space between pushing a congregation to think differently about an issue and settling into the routine of church life. Starting in the 1940s, white ministers in Richmond questioned their congregations' and the larger community's embrace of a segregated society. The pushback from fellow ministers, laypeople, and the general public highlights a moment where white Christians struggled with interpreting what it meant to follow Jesus. The internal struggle over opening public schools and their own churches on a desegregated basis revealed Christianity's simultaneous ability to support segregation and provide the grounds for tearing down the scaffold of the region's social practice.

Marion's sermon then highlighted where the tension over challenges to racial norms could occur within the church, even when everyone agreed that Jesus was the risen Christ. Using Douglas's novel as a starting point to talk about how ambition and wealth can get in the way of following Christ, he challenged a financially comfortable congregation to consider their loyalties to careers, ambition, and national pride. The sermon envisioned a world dedicated to Christ's example of self-sacrifice and service to fellow humans. "In a world," he exclaimed, "that seems in many ways to have gone mad—destructively insane—what we need are more Christians who, possessed heart and soul by their faith, will be willing to seem fools in the world's eyes in order to speak forth effectively the healing words of truth and soberness." His obsession involved an outward expression of engagement with the world generated from the knowledge of God's love for humanity. Marion's sermon affirmed the starting point of evangelical faith as personal piety but encouraged that faith to have an outward expression.

Marion laid out an argument that suggested the world was in need of Christians so totally committed to Christ that their focus would burn bright the light of Christ's love. "No Christian heart," he pointed out, "can ever give its best to the world unless it be a burning heart." Marion envisioned a church universal so alive that it could "be an effective force in molding tomorrow's world," if and only if it had "men and women obsessed, as it were by a magnificent devotion to the church." He outlined in the sermon the power of personal piety to transform the soul, but Marion also believed that Christians were called to be agents of God's work in the world. He drew the line clearly for a socially engaged faith. "A strong, intelligent, faithful church," Marion challenged, "with its fingers on the world's pulse, its mind on the world's problems, and its hands set manfully to serve the world's need—that sort of church will be a towering cathedral to inspire and guide mankind." With references to Nazis in Germany and imperialists in Japan, he contextualized a faith that paid attention to the world around it and noted that obsessions in themselves were dangerous because anyone can be passionate, but Marion argued that following Christ's example channeled the obsession. He was also willing to challenge the congregants to question their own patriotism during a time of war.

In a telling moment in the sermon, Marion framed his belief in the power of a magnificent obsession with Christ in terms that would look prophetic years later. The power of national pride can be seductive, as the nation would learn in the 1950s with the spectacle of Joseph McCarthy, and the pastor warned of a nation bending its image of God into itself. "The war," Marion noted, "more and more is becoming for us all, I realize, a rather magnificent obsession. Our patriotic zeal is a rising fever. The aims and goals of our nation are consuming more and more of our time and interest. Millions are willing to be fools for our flag, and this by and large,

I think, is all to the good." The problem occurred, he thought, when believers saw the vision of the nation overcoming the vision of God. "But fine as that [national] obsession may be," Marion stated, "it will be a sad day for our country and the world if we let it blot out or even weaken the still more magnificent obsession by when we are tied in loyalty and consecration to the Church of Christ." Marion, like Paul, saw the value of being a citizen of the state but allowed his faith to call into question its required loyalty. His willingness to challenge the congregation at a time of intense national pride revealed that in later years Marion would be willing to confront churches to think about other ways they may have been outside of God's vision.

After leaving Grace Covenant to become executive director of the Committee on Christian Relations for the Presbyterian Church in the United States (PCUS), Marion published an article in the *Yale Review* titled "Farewell, My Lovely Magnolias." In the article he argued that by holding on to traditions that "stymied" a generation of young southern leaders to think more critically about issues like Christianity and racial norms those capable minds would leave the region. "Our racial pattern," he wrote, "is so rigid, its daily compulsions are so at variance with our principles and our finer human instincts, and the atmosphere it sets up is so pervasive, that its repressive and stultifying effects are felt in practically all areas of our social life, making it harder for the typical thinking Southerner to be avowedly unorthodox and liberal, about anything, than perhaps similar placed individuals elsewhere in the country."[3] Though the article was a larger criticism of southerners and a call for them to think about why the region rejected dissenting voices that may have solutions to the South's problems, Marion's examples of why segregation harmed progress in the South suggested a white minster ready to take aim at the region's number one "bugaboo."[4]

It was the beginning of a nearly two-decade battle Marion waged against segregation both in public arenas as well as denominational and church settings. As the director of the Committee on Christian Relations he formulated most of the Presbyterian Church in the United States' social relations statements. Beginning in the spring of 1949, those pronouncements attacked segregation directly and the Presbyterian Church's role in supporting the social practice. The *Richmond News Leader* noted the report and quoted its finding: "'discrimination . . . is as doomed as human slavery,' according to a committee of Southern Presbyterian leaders." Marion's prophetic voice came through in the criticism for the Church to lead. "A church that tries to be neutral by keeping silent," the report stated, "or a church that resorts to compromise to save itself, will to that extent forfeit its redemptive power and influence among men."[5] One year later, he called for the abolition of segregation.[6] By 1957, Marion's ministerial cohort in the Richmond Ministers' Association (RMA), using language that Marion had used for almost a decade to condemn the practice, failed to give segregationists the most important justification they needed to continue to defend their position.

The "Magnificent Obsession" sermon held clues of his willingness to confront those who saw the world differently. Marion quizzed the congregation at Grace Covenant on the sanity of such an approach to blind faith. "Foolish," he asked them, "to put our Christianity first, come storm and fire? Foolish to believe the church can mold the world if only we dream and think and toil and pray?" The answer: "Perhaps! Yet that is the madness to which our Lord has commanded us." In a closing fit for the likes of Martin Luther King Jr. and Walter Rauschenbusch, Marion exclaimed, "For a mad world in which paganism has become an obsession for so many, nothing can be a true guide to *social salvation* but a church so great, so intense, so aflame for Christ and his way, that many about us will think us mad ever to have dreamed it."[7] Using language of personal conversion and devotional piety, he shifted the end result away from inner spiritual peace, though that was a goal, to an outward manifestation of social engagement. Faith in God, Marion argued in his sermon, meant doing God's will, which for him meant a desegregated church in a desegregated South.

John Marion's ministerial life suggests how a prophetic witness works in local congregations. Within the decade of his arrival in Richmond, he had moved from the largest Presbyterian congregation (Grace Covenant) in the South to a significant denominational position, and then back to pastoring a different, smaller congregation in Richmond. Marion's outspokenness on desegregation within southern Presbyterianism appeared to have cost him the director position. In 1950 he became pastor of a 150-member church, Bon Air Presbyterian, which had a close relationship with Union Theological Seminary in Richmond where Marion's advocacy had a willing audience. By 1955, and as a response to segregationists forming the Defenders of Liberty and State Sovereignty, a group sympathetic to desegregation formed the Virginia Council on Human Relations (VCHR), which served as a state-level extension of work done through the Southern Regional Council. Marion became its first executive director. He left the VCHR in 1958 to begin work for the newly formed United Presbyterian Church in North America, covering the southern region, in the area of human relations with a focus on racial issues. In the early 1960s, he moved his family and headquarters to Nashville, Tennessee. Movement away from the local pastorate does not suggest that those congregations disapproved of his position on desegregation. In fact, his most pointed comment on the subject came in a committee report to the General Assembly that condemned the denomination for not doing more to desegregate churches shortly before he assumed his duties at Bon Air. Marion's continued commitment to racial reconciliation indicated that he did not waiver in his intent that racial segregation in churches be seen as morally wrong.

Marion had willing partners in people like Aubrey Brown, editor of the magazine the *Presbyterian Outlook*, who also resided in Richmond and advocated for a desegregated church. Like Brown, Marion could effect broader change beyond the local congregation. It also meant, however, that strong voices for bringing about change in actual congregations had moved away from the source. The tendency to push too hard meant that job security, regardless of denominational polity, was fragile. As Marion's trajectory suggested, it was easier to confront when some distance could be gained. It was also true that moving beyond a single community to find like-minded believers created success for these reformers. Both of these realities also revealed how hard it would be to bring about change in a segregated society. Highlighting Marion frames this story in terms of privileging the prophetic voice. The civil rights movement, the narrative arc typically told, was on the correct side of history. Marion was advocating this position prior to the success, so some white southerners were enlightened and progressive. While John Marion is worthy of a biography, why does the arc bend to progressive political outcomes? Or for that matter, why do we think of churches in political terms at all? Prophetic voices help to move churches beyond the cultural strains that can entrap the faithful in social norms they believe God had formed. For every prophet, however, priestly voices ground the congregations in tradition and help fend off false prophets. Churches live between these two voices. To answer the questions, we must examine how Gunnar Myrdal's emphasis on ideal forms of church influenced our understanding of white congregations.

Gunnar Myrdal and White Christians

At the very moment Marion was preaching and ministering at Grace Covenant, Gunnar Myrdal released his findings on how racial constructions in the United States hindered the power and the promise of the American Dream, particularly among black Americans. *An American Dilemma* outlined the ways that "all men are created equal" fell short in a society based on inequality.[8] The victory of Allied forces against Germany and Japan almost a year after the publication of Myrdal's work also helped expose racial assumptions apparent in the United States. Fighting a war against the racism of the Nazi Party and Japanese notions of superiority, African Americans had served in a segregated military and had been treated as inferiors at home. The process, still peeling back layers today, became heightened in the decades following the end of the war.

As some African Americans were equally swept up in the expansion of the American economy, they began to exercise their economic clout and pushed back against the weight of the American contradiction of equality in the land of separation. Jim Crow, enforced by custom as much as law, created a category of second-class citizens. The power of what Myrdal termed the American Creed, a light of hope for generations, revealed the emptiness of the promise of a nation. This failure was not self-evident to white citizens in America. The dilemma suggested that the United States could only fulfill its potential when black Americans could experience the fruit of the nation's creed. As Myrdal noted, white Americans could and should have understood the power of racial constraints in the social structures that impeded progress for black citizens in a land of the free. Nowhere was this point more apparent to him than in white churches.

A part of Myrdal's personal life serves to highlight why that reading of the period, at least in Richmond, misses crucial elements of the civil rights struggle. On the day the US Supreme Court released its decision in *Brown*, Richmond area leaders had scheduled Myrdal to give public lectures on his work for the United Nations. Five days before the court released its opinion, Richmond newspapers reported, "Dr. Myrdal, Hurt, Can't Keep Two Richmond Dates." Having suffered a broken hip in an accident, Myrdal had to cancel his scheduled Cecil Scott Memorial Lecture for the Richmond Public Forum on Monday evening, May 17, 1954. He had also been asked to speak to the Richmond Area Community Council at the YWCA earlier that same afternoon. In both cases, Myrdal's presence in Richmond allowed him to talk about his work as the executive secretary for the United Nations Economic Committee for Europe.[9] Given the intimate network of collaborators in this kind of social organizing, Richmond leaders were aware of Myrdal's emphasis on social progressivism. His visit to Richmond highlighted the work of progressives in the city. Though Richmond would be home to some of the most sophisticated arguments for blocking the court's decision, the city also had individuals and groups working to bring about changes in social justice.

Given the forces advocating for desegregation of schools in Virginia, Myrdal might have escaped Richmond unscathed that day had he appeared since there was a muted response in the first few weeks after the decision. Segregationists were aware of the emphasis placed on social scientific studies, including Myrdal's *American Dilemma*, during oral arguments before the US Supreme Court the previous fall. The psychological and sociological effects of segregation on black children, found notably in Kenneth Clark's work as well as Myrdal's, meant that the court would have to rest its decision on nonlegal precedent. This shift worried some segregationists and they hoped for a split vote by the court.[10]

The court's unanimous decision caught segregationists in Virginia off guard. Within a year, however, those advocating resistance, including James J. Kilpatrick, marshaled their forces to argue the court had used sociological and psychological studies instead of legal precedent to upend "separate but equal" in public education. Kilpatrick wanted to argue that segregationists' interpretation of the Constitution meant that precedent in law required the court to uphold "separate but equal." Since the court had introduced social scientific findings into its decision, the court had overstepped its authority and a process of nullification, open to the states, allowed any state the right to ignore the ruling.[11]

Myrdal had come to the United States in 1938 to begin a Carnegie Foundation study on race and racism in American society. Published in 1944, the wide-ranging text examined the "paradoxical" reality of a democratic society that lacked universal suffrage. The nation, he argued, had a set of principles by which it "ought" to live. Myrdal also connected the American ideal to roots in Protestant Christianity. Pointing to a "spirit" of freedom through religious liberty, he suggested that the democratic ideal found in Protestant denominations in the states reinforced the creed's dependence upon religious ideals. Christianity in the United States, Myrdal noted, created a spirit of democracy as it simultaneously built walls of separation both within religious communities and in the larger culture.

A problem with focusing on an ideal position is that it easily reveals the shortcomings of reality rather than point a way forward. With an ideal as the example, hypocrisy is easily visible. The logic goes something like this: if all churches just embraced their emphasis on liberty, then the nation could move toward racial justice. Opening a door that has captured the imagination of those studying white southerners, Myrdal laid a substantial part of the blame for poor race relations at the feet of white Christians.[12]

In *An American Dilemma*, however, Myrdal advanced a sophisticated understanding of the purpose of churches in any society, but his emphasis on the ideal in terms of segregation narrowed the interpretative lens. The study stressed the conserving social nature of religious communities. The work acknowledged the important role that religion plays in grounding a society by predicting that future sociologists would be struck by the religious nature of Americans even as "the process of progressive secularization" continued in the western world.[13] Churches, Myrdal conceded, serve a social function that should indicate why they do not always lead in social reform. Black churches, he added, preserve basic elements of the social structure of the black communities and therefore play a significant role in shaping those communities' identity. This point explained why black churches had "not become an institution that led the opposition to the caste system."[14] For Myrdal, this acceptance of the American creed found a strange outlet in conservative responses to change, including in churches. The study's emphasis on religion as a conserver of social order meant that a sociological framework explained why churches moved so slowly on desegregation.

Given the success of evangelical Protestantism in the American South during the one hundred years preceding Myrdal's study, religious leaders emphasized transforming the culture but often within culturally acceptable ways. Examples of this odd relationship found expression in two different social issues: prohibition against alcohol and segregation on public carriers. The temperance movement fought to dismantle a complex social system and garnered widespread popularity in southern Protestant churches. Attempts to end racial segregation on public transport, however, failed to gain enough momentum to overturn local ordinances, even where church leaders in places like Richmond were vocal supporters of desegregation. This idea meant that all churches could be in a place to challenge social norms, but they were just as likely to maintain the status quo. In the case of prohibition, organizers, even white religious leaders, could play on the racially constructed fear of black men, alcohol, and white women. Myrdal acknowledged the value that churches give to advancing a culture by stabilizing it, but the ideal church community looked more desegregated than what he found in the United States.

As Marion's story showed, there were voices crying in the wilderness, but they struggled against social forces that reinforced racial norms within theological language. By shifting the focus backward in time, the internal discussions of white religious leaders and congregations reveal how varied the responses by white Christians in Richmond were as they struggled with themselves to make sense of the rapid changes underway.[15] Part of the reason for this lack of attention on the earlier period surrounding *Brown* involved how historians have interpreted Myrdal's work.[16] The emphasis on the ideal congregation's relationship to desegregation has meant that all of the work done by white ministers during the 1940s and 1950s was a failure because churches ultimately failed to desegregate themselves in the 1960s or beyond. "Going on record" appeared to alter little in the struggle over desegregation.

If Myrdal's study has become the framework for scholars to understand the failure of white Christians to engage segregation, it also serves as starting point for understanding white churches' and Christians' responses to massive resistance and the civil rights movement. The grounding of religious practice in social norms creates the space for calling them into question and only insiders have the authority to make those challenges. Even as Myrdal pointed out the failure of white churches to lead in desegregation, young white ministers in the South like John Marion began to challenge their churches' approach to segregation. Though their numbers appeared small and often scattered across the southern landscape, something segregationists needed southerners to believe, these ministers built extensive networks and confronted the cultural forms of Christianity, including the perceived biblical command to segregate the races. In Richmond, their numbers were significant, and when pushed publicly, they showed their commitment to a desegregated order. Myrdal's hope that white churches could lead a way forward on racial justice already had ministers on the ground ready to lead the charge. As early as the 1930s, the Fellowship of Southern Churchmen (FSC) encouraged ministers to challenge their church members to see segregation as antithetical to the gospel.[17] Formed as a way for ministers to share ideas about ecumenical dialogue and social justice, the FSC would morph several times over the thirty-year period from its founding until the mid-1960s. Though its broader emphasis would remain on economic issues, the issue of race relations came to animate almost all of its activities.

This loose network of like-minded ministers helped those who participated in the group's programming to know they were not alone in the struggle. Given that the FSC also advocated for thorny issues such as economic justice and the use of atomic energy, this group of ministers gave expression to what the social gospel movement looked like in the American South with an emphasis on addressing social systems in tandem with personal choices as sinful. Anyone railing against economic and racial injustice during the 1940s in the South would have cut a lonely figure. The organization's annual meetings helped these ministers come together to make public stands (pronouncements) about how the gospel influenced the way believers engaged their world—the kind of obsession John Marion talked about in his sermon. The FSC's strong commitment to hold desegregated meetings meant every time they gathered they were a witness against the racial Christianity of the South. During the spring of 1946, they descended on Richmond, Virginia, to hold meetings at Second Presbyterian Church and Richmond Central YMCA, including the cultural taboo of desegregated formal meals at the latter.

The congregation at Second Presbyterian had seen a significant shift on the racial question since their longtime pastor Moses Hoge died in 1899. Second Presbyterian Church sits in an area that during the Civil War was on the city's western edge. From the war to the turn of the century, Confederate Rev. Dr. Moses Hoge served the congregation. His dedication to the Confederate cause was so strong that Hoge was asked to be an emissary to England to secure supplies and to negotiate England's entry into the war on the side of the Confederacy.[18] When Judah P. Benjamin (the Secretary of War and a friend of Hoge) and the rest of the Confederate government retreated from the city on a Sunday morning, Hoge interrupted the worship service to announce that he had to leave the city as well.[19] The use by the FSC of this particular church less than fifty years after Hoge's death showed how far ministerial thinking had moved on racial issues in some circles. Rev. Olin Currie had become the pastor of Second Presbyterian in the 1940s and was part of the FSC, working with Nelle Morton to bring the meeting to Richmond. The location of the church across the street from the YMCA, which along with the YWCA had established a practice of desegregated facilities across the United States by the late 1940s, helped in making the decision.[20] Currie's ability to use the church for the meeting signaled that some Presbyterian ministers in Richmond were willing to lead their congregations toward a broader understanding of desegregation. The Richmond edition of the *Afro-American* called attention to the meeting and noted that the group was an "interdenominational, interracial movement of men and women interested in applying the resources of the Christian faith to the critical and complex problems affecting the welfare of the county [*sic*] and the people."[21] The ability to move beyond denominational lines would be important in the decade ahead as ministers attempted to change racial sensibilities.

At the supper meeting of the group at the YMCA, the assembly passed a resolution calling on all religious people in the United States to open their hearts and their churches to people of any race. The resolution called on "churches, synagogues and cathedrals to join [the FSC] in combating the evil designs of the vendors of hate and distrust who would set man against man, playing upon his pride, his pretensions to power, his economic insecurity, his political fears and his religious sectarianism." The statement challenged southern churchgoers to be critical of the society, both its regional and American forms, in which they lived.[22] Here Myrdal's observation about "going on record" suggests that resolutions change little about the social issues they address. Since there is almost no way to enforce the proclamations, scholars have noted they carry no effect. Pronouncements, however, do change things. In part, they signal to believers the direction their leaders are taking on an issue. This approach may not show immediate results, which we often look for, but in this case the resolution attempted to call white congregations to a different vision of church life. The line between prophetic witness and priestly function, however, is a thin one. The conviction to push forward would not be shared by everyone, even when the meeting's purpose was celebrated as a sign of the coming kingdom of God.

The editor of the (Richmond) *Afro-American* left little to chance and reinforced the importance of the meeting. "A new and powerful movement . . . ," the editor wrote, "composed of Christian men and women from sixteen Southern States, came to our fair city last week and forced the practice of democracy in at least a part of Richmond for two full days." Particularly, the editorial suggested "the pastor and elders of that congregation [Second Presbyterian]" understood "that it can open its doors to ALL, regardless of race, color or creed, without fear of inviting disaster."[23] In this plea the power of the confrontations of the 1960s becomes clear. African Americans, as Myrdal's study suggested, needed desegregated spaces to experience the American dream. Desegregated settings did not necessarily mean an integrated relationship. Access meant opportunity for creating networks and social capital, but in a more important way, it meant acceptance. Congregations straddle the line between public and private because of their openness to new members; all have rules for full participation but allow people to enter without meeting certain criteria. In the Jim Crow South, skin tone created a visible standard and white Christians had begun to think of their worship space as a place to be protected. As the editorial noted, white Christians in Richmond should have seen allies in the fight to bring positive moral change to the city. Instead, as in other areas across the region, white citizens in Richmond held more firmly to social assumptions about race mixing than as an opportunity for growth with black Christians. The editorial revealed an interesting tension for the FSC. The plea from the editor called on the congregation to see that if black Christians came into worship nothing bad would happen. The meeting, however, simply used the building space without engaging the congregation's racial assumptions.

After congratulating those present on their display of true democracy and warning them about the road ahead, the editorial concluded, "if they are possessed of the intestinal fortitude, the Christian zeal and the will to victory that we feel they have, they can create in the South a church worthy of the name—one which will help this benighted section to find its soul."[24] The interracial group's meeting had changed little at Second Presbyterian Church, but it also revealed the inherent illogic of racial etiquette in the South. Though none of the African American members of the FSC would ask to become members of Second Presbyterian Church, in part because they were not residents of the city but also because they already were members of other congregations, social custom forbade their presence in a public setting delineated as "white," which included churches. If the church wanted to invite black citizens into the building, it could legally do so. Social conventions, however, prevented members of the congregation from considering nonwhite members. This perception of what a desegregated church looked like caused many, including Myrdal, to emphasize the failure of white churches to lead toward the nation's creed. More than a decade later, the kneel-in campaigns showed how far white congregations were willing to go to keep their spaces segregated. The *Afro-American* editorial pointed out why courage on the part of white Richmond Christians mattered: only they had the power to change the racial climate. As Olin Currie's example showed, there were ministers ready to lead, and even some members of churches willing to follow, but their struggle in the 1940s and 1950s had little to do with desegregated congregations and everything to do with convincing fellow white Christians that a desegregated society was part of God's plan for the nation. The result of the meeting suggests that had its message been heeded the confrontational aspects of the civil rights movement would have been unnecessary. The FSC's small presence in the larger society, however, meant that it could be ignored, so confrontation became the only way to force white Christians to see that their racial sensibilities hindered the work of the kingdom of God.

Second Presbyterian Church membership and at least some members of its session board did take exception to the gathering in their building. Nelle Morton, general secretary of the FSC, sent fellow member John Ellison, president of Virginia Union University, a letter advising him of some pushback Currie had received from his congregation. In his response, Ellison noted that he had not heard about any problems at Second Presbyterian. Since Morton had suggested that Ellison send Currie a note, Ellison pointed out that he was confident Currie could handle "whatever unpleasant reactions may come from any member of his church or official board" in an effective manner. Ellison added, however, that he also understood "how much it means to have words of encouragement of those for whom and with whom we worked in order to make the Kingdom of God real in this world."[25] It would not be the last time a pastor at Second Presbyterian felt pressure after encouraging congregants to see the problem of segregation in religious terms.

Years later, Nelle Morton would note that the FSC's good work on racial justice and civil rights meant that from the mid-1950s forward, discussion about race overshadowed other work the FSC attempted to accomplish. The Richmond meeting revealed that process was underway before the 1950s. Indeed, the public resolution frames the issue more broadly than racial discrimination. The FSC's leadership body, which crafted the resolution "Guideposts for Action," wanted to encourage its members to engage two issues in particular: the important role religious leaders could play in ending discrimination and the use of atomic energy as a force for destruction.[26] In this way, the FSC worked from a regional perspective to an international perspective while fostering a need for broader economic justice. The race issue was one part of a larger project for the FSC. Richmond's edition of the *Afro-American* narrowed the scope of the FSC's work, emphasizing a point Myrdal had emphasized two years earlier: white churches failed to lead by example in creating a desegregated society.

Since few white Richmonders read the *Afro-American*, they could ignore the plea, and that scenario pointed to a growing problem concerning desegregation. The request for equal access meant something different from integration. As Jane Dailey has pointed out, as far back as the Readjuster period in the 1870s and 1880s, some white Virginians had heard the word *integration* as a form of race mixing, or miscegenation.[27] African Americans, however, used the term to suggest that fairness and human decency demanded equal access. By the 1940s, and in the immediate afterglow of victory in the race war over Nazi Germany, the custom of segregation overwhelmed every aspect of life in the American South. The contradiction so apparent to Myrdal a decade earlier had only become more intense. Calls for a desegregated society, by the FSC, or a desegregated congregation, from the pages of the *Afro-American*, meant little to white southerners, even as they pointed to the hypocrisy regarding loving one's neighbor.

The FSC's approach to race relations revealed two important emphases in the post–World War South concerning Christianity. Whether congregations were ready or not, some white southern ministers and denominational leaders felt compelled to press their members not only to think about racial issues but also to see how churches could lead in bringing about economic justice. Theological training in the 1930s and 1940s had prepared a different type of minister from that of the nineteenth century, and the change would have long-term repercussions in the South. The conflict over desegregation signaled tensions within Christian denominations over how to interpret scripture in light of current political contexts that would remain visible for the remainder of the twentieth century and into the next. In this way, the FSC's work suggested the way ecumenical groups of like-minded people tended to be vehicles for advancing progressive voices publicly. The group also highlighted, though unintentionally, the limits of its approach. When ministerial associations spoke, white Christians in Richmond could choose to ignore or dismiss them. The "race problem" was a "Negro" problem and white ministers could preach and "go on record" but their members could also walk away. Because many historians have framed success in Myrdal's terms, they have missed a crucial piece of this story. The amount of groundwork white ministers and lay people put in place from the 1930s into the 1960s meant change was coming.

Defenders of massive resistance had not anticipated the shift in opinion among white ministers concerning segregation, even as those ministers had started signaling the change. In spring 1953, three Richmond ministerial associations merged to form the Richmond Ministers' Association when a biracial organization (Protestant Ministers' Association) joined forces with two white ministerial groups (Richmond Ministers' Union and Interdenominational Ministerial Alliance), illustrating an unprecedented show of interracial cooperation in Richmond. The new group's constitution listed as one of its goals "to manifest the essential oneness of the ministers of Richmond and vicinity in Jesus Christ, and to foster fellowship and mutual understanding among the members." Rev. C. Emerson Smith, chairman of interracial work for the Virginia Council of Churches, said the merger was the "culmination of a long period of increasing fellowship and cooperation between the Negro and white ministers of Richmond." He believed the organization would bring about renewed hope for race relations. Smith said it is "an expression of the Christian doctrine of the brotherhood of man and it will make possible a greater effectiveness in working for the Kingdom of God in Richmond."[28]

One month later, on April 27, 1953, Rev. Clyde V. Hickerson, pastor of Barton Heights Baptist Church since 1944, became the first elected president of the new association. The other officers were Rev. H. A. Parker, Leigh Street Methodist (white), vice president; Rev. Irving Elligan, All Souls Presbyterian (black), secretary; and Rev. James S. Gupton, Battery Park Christian (white), treasurer. In their first meeting at the Central YMCA in Richmond, Edward E. Haddock, mayor of Richmond and lay leader in the Virginia Conference (Methodist), addressed the group and asked them to give serious study to the "parking problem" caused by overflowing downtown churches. He also urged them to keep their membership interested in "good government." Haddock told the body to "stress law observance, particularly to reduce the 'constant picture' of traffic accidents."[29] He would go on to play a crucial role in the massive resistance debates in the Virginia General Assembly, becoming a voice for desegregation supporters. His relationship to these ministers and lay leaders would play an important part of undermining segregationists' arguments.[30]

Within the first seven months of its existence, the RMA displayed a character that would guide it through the early period of desegregation unrest. If Richmonders thought the ministers would focus solely on pedestrian issues like parking, they were sorely mistaken. In fact, the nature of the organization as an interracial body dedicated to giving black and white ministers equal footing should have indicated otherwise. By November 1953, the association confronted desegregation of public transportation and public assemblies in the city. The group voted to petition the state legislature in its January meeting to "repeal laws requiring racial segregation on common carriers and in public assemblies in the State." The group's civic committee—chaired by Rev. W. L. Ransome, pastor of First Baptist Church, South Richmond (a black church) and editor of the *Baptist Herald*—led the petition drive. The decision placed the ministerial association at the center of the public debate over desegregation for the first time. Although the position accorded with other pronouncements by several denominations and the Virginia Council of Churches, the Richmond ministers made clear that Christian faith and a segregated society could not sustain each other. Rather than simply taking a rhetorical position, the ministers intended to affect public policy.[31] With this first step, the RMA entered into a growing debate over religion's place in the political world, which climaxed in its Statement of Conviction in 1957.

The ministers had picked an unpopular issue for their first foray into segregation politics. Virginius Dabney, the editor of the *Richmond Times-Dispatch* and a quintessential white southern liberal, had signaled the need for desegregating public transportation during World War II to the deafening sound of silence. While Dabney thought of himself as a liberal, his motives have been called into question. Christopher Silver and John Moeser have suggested that Dabney might have been motivated by a fear of outside agitators exploiting the issue of African American discontent to their advantage, particularly in light of the release of the Durham Statement.[32] Regardless of the Richmond editor's motivation, Dabney's opinion largely fell on deaf ears. A similar fate awaited the RMA's petition on desegregated public transportation. But the early public work of the RMA revealed the road it would take when the fight over desegregation heated up after 1956.

Having preached about confronting Christianity's loyalty to cultural norms, John Marion emerged as a vocal and committed advocate of desegregated hearts and institutions within the RMA.[33] Marion's address to the group in December 1953, only one month after the decision to petition the state legislature regarding desegregation of public transportation, should have signaled to white Richmonders a shift in tone regarding segregation by Richmond ministers. Having already publicly criticized denominational bureaucrats in 1950 for not publicly supporting desegregation of graduate schools,[34] he spoke to the group with an address titled "A Southerner Looks at Segregation." Marion minced no words calling segregation a "social sickness" that needed to be addressed firmly and directly. "The time has come," he admonished his ministerial colleagues, "for a sounder, bolder and more effective therapy. The time has come to see that we can no more meet and solve this problem by ignoring it in the classroom or the pulpit than we can wipe out the menace of communism by the same head-in-the-sand tactics." Asserting what Aubrey Brown, editor of the *Presbyterian Outlook*, later called the moral "higher plain [*sic*]," Marion continued: "We have now come to a critical period when more of us will have to start saying to all who are prepared to listen, that much current talk about states' rights and the perils of legislation doesn't take us down to the primary and most important issue of all. The basic issue is not economic or political or psychological—it is moral." He rejected the notion that the end of segregation meant "enforced" race mixing. Claiming that black people really just wanted "full and equal civil rights in such fields as education, employment, housing and medical services," Marion said that giving such rights "will not require the intimate social acceptance of undesirable individuals of any color by the squeamish members of any majority group."[35]

Few people took notice of his comments published in Richmond's newspapers. The *Richmond News Leader* published the story about the address on page 15, and although the *Richmond Times-Dispatch* ran it as a front-page story, response was nonexistent. Ministers like John Marion were creating little doubt about the sinful nature of segregation. The lack of response from readers to the ministers' criticism cannot be fully explained, since the RMA was openly engaged in a public debate over desegregation. If Gunnar Myrdal's work on race in America had called for white churches to lead the way, there were signs in the 1940s and early 1950s that suggested there were ministers ready to lead.

The time and distance between Myrdal's work on race and the desegregation struggle in the late 1950s reveal a great deal about how America's "dilemma" situated itself in almost every facet of American life. Although only a small part of the overall study, Myrdal suggested that white American Protestant churches appeared to exhibit the greatest hypocrisy toward liberty of the soul in a segregated order. While it is true that the historical record suggests that the best ministers and some churches did was "go on record," a closer examination of churches and church leaders in one place may help us better understand the power of "going on record" and the extent to which advocates of desegregation were going before, during, and after *Brown*.

In Richmond and elsewhere in the South, segregationists faced opposition from white religious leaders and laypeople as the example of the Fellowship of Southern Churchmen revealed. While the overt political moves of the period indicate a reinforcement of the status quo, there were voices calling out to change the system. When James Kilpatrick amplified his call for nullification of the US Supreme Court's ruling in *Brown*, Richmond ministers, many of whom were present for the FSC meeting in 1946, challenged the politics of massive resistance. It is easy to dismiss these people as marginal players in the unfolding events of desegregation. This localized study gives us a better sense of how many folks engaged the process and how much influence they exerted. Indeed, Numan Bartley highlighted the work of the RMA and its protracted struggle to shame Virginia's General Assembly and Governor to rescind the "massive resistance" laws passed in 1956 to circumvent *Brown*. Besides cursory references to the group and its activity in 1957, however, there has been no study of the ministers or the organization. By examining the work of the RMA and the ministers who have left a record of their activities we can see patterns of ministerial engagement in the political process and the results of that tussle, even as these ministers continued to lead segregated worship services.

A Way Forward

The inherent trap for overvaluing the prophetic voice in the life of religious communities (as I have just done in highlighting the work of the RMA in its response to segregation issues) is that we undervalue the social cohesion that churches provide as "moral communities," which Myrdal had noted.[36] Rather than see one response as appropriate and the other inappropriate, we need to understand that both responses exist within and sustain religious communities.[37] Some black ministers were prophetic in advocating for civil rights during the early-to-midtwentieth century, for example, but they were also either remarkably quiet about or vocally advocated Victorian values in their understanding of the family and the role of women in the church. Though African American churches often failed to address the role of women within their communities at the time, this attitude speaks to the general tension that congregations and religious leaders live in as they engage the world around them. The visible oppression of segregation and the growing sense that there were specific moments to act on that issue brought clarity to the prophetic witness, even if not everyone could see it at the time.

The public stance for civil rights did not necessarily move African American congregations toward the ideal *within* the church in part because religious leaders would disagree over the ideal as it related to women in the 1960s. This example suggests that we see the prophetic tied to larger societal changes, or perhaps that is how we have come to see it. Prophets, however, only make sense of their particular moral communities internally, and even then they are not always heeded.

Given the tendency to emphasize the prophetic ideal, there appears to be a need to develop a framework for understanding the complexities of local congregations and individuals who make up those communities. Charles Marsh paved a way forward in his theological history of Freedom Summer. In *God's Long Summer*, he told the story of the intense struggle for voting rights in Mississippi through five theological biographies to examine how people appropriated their theological visions toward the sociopolitical events in Mississippi during 1964. The pairings are important because the "theological drama" found in the lives of Klan preacher Sam Bowers and civil rights activist Fannie Lou Hamer reveals that their positions start at similar hermeneutical points—the faithfulness of God and the ordering of society. Their interpretative conclusions, however, diverge into emphasizing the power of God's justice on earth (Hamer) and prioritizing the purity of God's righteousness (Bowers).[38] Both saw God as just but differed on how that just God envisioned human interaction.

The other three biographies highlight various possible responses between Christianity and political engagement. Interestingly, the position of white pastor Douglas Hudgins in the group highlights a pious disengagement with the struggle, something that happens when ministers fail to lead in social movement flashpoints. Marsh was clear that Hudgins's position allowed Bowers's segregationist theology to be an acceptable alternative to desegregation.[39] He lays the blame for Sam Bowers's hate-filled success at the feet of Hudgins's "closed" theology. Marsh's theological reading of Hudgins does not follow Myrdal's sociological ideal, but the use of sociological and theological readings of the events of 1964 came to the same conclusion: leading white preachers had the ability to alter the events if they had chosen to do so. The inclusion of Ed King—who worked tirelessly as an activist for civil rights both in churches and society—in the group reinforces this idea of prophetic engagement. Interestingly, Marsh acknowledged how individuals held nuanced positions regarding racial categories even as they argued for civil rights. Hamer could embrace a desegregated kingdom of God but not an integrated home. Her displeasure with interracial dating and support for "traditional sexual ethics" suggests that a biblical worldview can hold multiple frames of reference at once.[40]

Marsh's sensitive reading of theological perspectives in relationship to the political events of Freedom Summer helps us understand individual theological outlooks. What happened when congregations and denominations carried out this kind of theological drama? Even during the events of the 1960s, historians tried to figure out a lack of leadership among white congregations surrounding the civil rights movement. In most cases, Myrdal's emphasis on the ideal became the pattern. The literature surrounding white religious leaders, congregations, and denominations has been growing in the past few years. Early attempts to understand these conversations focused on single denominations or large para-church organizations like the National Council of Churches.[41] More recently, there have been works that focus on a narrow subject like a particular city or congregation.[42]

Marsh also examined life within religious communities as the restless younger generation of activists, both black and white, pushed for greater opportunities and freedom. Marsh recounts the tumultuous decade of the 1960s that began with student sit-ins at lunch counters and kneel-ins at churches in southern cities, then saw the violent deaths of John and Robert Kennedy as well as Martin Luther King Jr., and ended with the escalation of the war in Southeast Asia. Confrontation warrants spectacle, but what happened when churches were not being pushed from the outside? Theological drama unfolds outside the headlines as often as it does in the public disputes over social policy or doctrine. We find an equally important story in the mundane life of congregations and denominations as they try to make sense of a world changing around them.

In this study of Richmond, I examine the struggle *within* and *between* white religious individuals and organizations, usually in conversation with black individuals and organizations. Richmond in this case, as it already has in this chapter, serves as both a character and a backdrop in the narrative. When this occurs in the pages that follow, the geography of place recedes in the discussion and Richmond becomes an idea, home to important institutions in the debate. Since segregation was both an idea and a practice, the contested space both public and private reveals how religion serves to support white assumptions about race while also challenging those assumptions. The period reveals how white Christians in Richmond wrestled with the ideal that Myrdal pointed toward. Herein lies the problem, or at least one of them, for historians of the period. What is the ideal? For Richmonders who resisted any change, the ideal involved a world set right and ordered by God, even a segregated one. Often scripture could defend this position, but just as often these Richmonders would rest their arguments on social norms or "just the way things are" kind of thinking. In the late 1950s and early 1960s, this approach would find expression in what Stephen Haynes called spectacles of exclusion. In the early 1950s, however, there was little need for exclusion in churches since there were few examples of direct action against white churches. In 1960 the contested landscape, however, changed when young black college students, joining the example set in Greensboro, North Carolina, began the sit-in campaign at department stores in Richmond, and were joined by white seminary students from Union Theological Seminary in Richmond. In the 1960s the confrontation would move to churches themselves, but those spectacles created a lasting impression about white congregations. The historical memory jumps from the antebellum defense of slavery to deacons standing at church doors keeping black college students from entering the sanctuary. Those moments of conflict during the civil rights movement in places like Georgia, Mississippi, and Tennessee, where white congregations' resistance to change were caught on film and televised or published in newspapers and magazines, have been etched onto the American psyche. In 1960 Weatherford Memorial Baptist Church, however, took out an advertisement in the *Richmond Times-Dispatch* announcing that by congregational vote its door were open to all in the city regardless of skin color. This move by a white congregation in Richmond suggests that we have more to uncover about religion and race in the American South. By examining Richmond during the decade that precedes the confrontation to desegregate congregations, we better understand that choices made years earlier affected how churches responded in the 1960s. The internal debates these Christians had during the decade reveal a great deal about how they were communities of both exclusion and embrace.[43]

Though religious historians have debunked the captivity thesis, the fact that churches remained the final visible reminder of segregated life in America allowed white congregations to be understood in narrow terms. Church relocation in the face of "white flight" or public exclusions of young African Americans from worship support that understanding, but the telling of the particular stories in particular places reshapes that interpretation. By asking big questions in small places, we may begin to better understand the nuanced responses by white ministers and congregations to the desegregation debates in the 1950s and 1960s.

2
IT WAS ONLY A MATTER OF TIME

Just to the north of Richmond's downtown area, across a ravine from the all-black neighborhood of Jackson Ward, and just south of Ginter Park where Union Theological Seminary at Richmond was located sat James Barton's little neighborhood, Barton Heights. Created in the 1880s as an attractive suburb for white city residents to escape the bustle of downtown, the neighborhood had grown so rapidly by the turn of the century that the city of Richmond annexed it and made its residents part of the city tax base. By the 1920s, five white congregations were firmly established in the neighborhood. By the 1950s, however, its racial composition looked quite different. The dramatic change within the area highlighted how racial transitions in Richmond's housing areas made the prospects of court-ordered desegregation problematic for white residents. In Barton Heights the rapid shift from white neighborhood to black neighborhood meant that white and black children could attend school together since white and black families in the 1950s lived in proximity to one another. At the same moment, those five white congregations experienced enough additional growth that each discussed plans to move from the neighborhood. Only one would be in its Barton Heights location in 1960, the other church buildings having been purchased by equally denominationally affiliated black congregations.

Although the five congregations in Barton Heights were responding to the changing landscape of suburban development in 1954, the neighborhood identity remained "white." Except for the Catholic students, white children at Barton Heights Baptist; Church of the Epiphany, Episcopal; Overbrook Presbyterian; and Barton Heights Methodist continued to attend the neighborhood schools. Church members were keenly aware that Richmond's black residents were moving across imaginary boundaries and into white neighborhoods. As long as schools remained segregated, however, black children in the area would still have to journey back into black neighborhoods to attend "Negro" schools. By the early 1950s, the legal team at the National Association for the Advancement of Colored People (NAACP), headed by Thurgood Marshall, began the final push to desegregate public education at the primary and secondary levels. Neighborhood schools became the contested arenas over desegregation. Since churches could abandon their neighborhoods as their members moved out, the conflict in the 1950s over schools and public spaces allowed individual congregations to escape direct confrontation. Religious leaders, however, engaged the school question, and in the process revealed something about how nuanced religious responses to social issues could be.

After their success in dismantling segregation in graduate schools in the 1940s, the NAACP lawyers turned their attention to secondary education. With little fanfare, and less attention, the NAACP in Virginia began building a test case in Pulaski County, in southwestern Virginia.[1] What the NAACP lawyers in Virginia were unprepared for was a student protest that erupted in 1951 Farmville, Virginia, over conditions in the black senior high school. Oliver Hill, one of the two lead NAACP attorneys in Virginia, received a tip that informed him the NAACP lawyers needed to stop by Prince Edward County to investigate the students' activities.[2] On their way to Pulaski they decided to stop in Farmville; the side trip forced the Virginia branch of the NAACP to change their plans, and the Prince Edward County case became one of the cases bundled together in the US Supreme Court's landmark ruling in *Brown v. Board of Education*.[3]

The early reaction by white southerners to the court's decision was mixed. In Richmond, a number of voices supported the court's decision, including several editors of denominational periodicals. The five responses made by these editors in light of larger statewide denominational and regional issues helps our understanding of the period around *Brown* as it relates to theological sentiments in Virginia. Religious editors articulated personal convictions within the context of denominational or hierarchical attitudes. While the bulk of a religious newspaper provided information about denominational life, in the case of *Brown* religious papers revealed how editors positioned their own convictions within larger structures and how they made sense of the order within their religious frameworks. None of the editors ignored the court's decision, lending their opinions to the shaping of religious discussion in Richmond and Virginia, and in the case of one paper in the larger region, concerning *Brown*.

The US Supreme Court's decision in *Brown* provided external pressure for white religious southerners to engage their theological suppositions to segregation. Without legal support for the justification of segregation, white Christians disclosed how their religious beliefs aligned with their political beliefs. They could no longer say that they disliked the treatment of black people but could do nothing about social customs. In the weekly and monthly periodicals, some religious leaders used at least two approaches to help believers live out how to love one's neighbor. These strategies took the form of sermon illustrations as a way to condition congregations to the idea of desegregation and a new emphasis on actual desegregated meetings of black and white congregations in the form of Race Relation Sunday events. Both methods helped white congregations think about racial issues differently without changing any of their patterns of segregated behavior.

There were, however, other white leaders who focused on drawing individuals into communities of radical living rather than changing the structures of society. Clarence Jordan at Koinonia Farms in Americus, Georgia, and Sherwood Eddy at the Delta (Bolivar County) and Providence (Holmes County) Farms in Mississippi were two examples. Both cooperatives created a prophetic model of racial and economic reconciliation without requiring congregations or the society around them to change. The radical piety of these men and organizations placed transformation within the believer's heart, hoping to alter society through witness. In both forms, the Fellowship of Southern Churchmen provided an outlet for clergy who were ready to challenge the status quo.

After *Brown*, however, white religious people in the South could no longer speak about their faith without exposing the inconsistency between the equality found in the gospel and the court-rejected inequality of public education, a point Myrdal had made almost a decade earlier. In the immediate aftermath of the decision, five religious editors in Richmond spoke with a variety of voices to their constituents regarding desegregation of public schools. Black Baptists and white Presbyterians read their editors' pushes for a fully desegregated order, including churches. White Baptists and Methodists found their editors unsympathetic to the court's decision, but the two editors approached the ruling with different understandings about how to proceed. In both cases, congregations would not need to desegregate. Catholics in Richmond had a bishop who desegregated their parochial schools in tandem with the court's decision, which ran counter to the public position of the most recognizable segregationist Catholic in Richmond, James J. Kilpatrick, the editor of the *Richmond News Leader*. These five editors elucidate the broad continuum of religious responses to *Brown*. In doing so, these editorial voices reveal the complex role Christianity plays when it engages in social debate. Rather than simply going on record, the editors outlined how Christians could understand the court's ruling in light of their faith. In the process, they also revealed competing visions for how the church functions in the world.

NAACP School Strategy and Virginia

After high-profile victories over segregated graduate school education in the South, the NAACP turned its attention to unequal educational opportunities for younger black children. Though black schools in Richmond did not have the horrendous physical conditions found in some of Virginia's rural areas, there was a sense that education for African American children reinforced notions of inferiority. As the city's public schools system busied itself building equalization schools, the curricular emphasis remained on trade and menial skill education. Rev. Robert Taylor remembered being shown the construction work on a new black high school, Armstrong High School, and inquired about the school's pedagogical focus. Without blinking, the superintendent replied that it would emphasize vocational training.[4] Even if white school systems equalized their physical plants for black teachers and students, their racialized notion of intellectual ability kept African Americans' access to opportunity unequal.

Events in Farmville, Virginia, a small municipality about sixty miles southwest of Richmond in Prince Edward County, became a catalyst for changing the social world of all Virginians and, through the court's decision, the South. Black students in Farmville, led by Barbara Johns (who was the sixteen-year-old niece of Rev. Vernon Johns, the preacher who preceded Martin Luther King Jr. at Dexter Avenue Baptist Church), had called for a strike at Moton High School to highlight the abysmal learning conditions in the "separate" black school.[5]

Prince Edward County, part of Virginia's Fourth Congressional District, was home to Senator Harry F. Byrd Sr.'s "machine" and the machine's most loyal support. In the early 1960s, it would also epitomize lengths that segregationist politicians would go to for massive resistance and ultimately the futility of that movement. Prince Edward County along with its neighbors from the James River at Richmond's southern border to the North Carolina border make up Virginia's "Southside." The black population in this region, which incorporates the northern reaches of the South's "Black Belt," almost equaled white people (167,139 and 171,211, respectively) in 1950.[6] Prince Edward County, and places like it all over the South, needed "separate but equal" schools, the argument went, because demographics blurred the legal color line. The county had two high schools, and a desegregated system would place black and white children in classes with one another based on school assignment plans.

One Richmond resident of growing prominence in the segregationist camp noted the emerging conflict inherent in the NAACP's legal strategy. James J. Kilpatrick succeeded Douglas Southall Freeman—noted biographer of George Washington and Robert E. Lee—as the editor of Richmond's evening newspaper, the *Richmond News Leader*, in 1951. In his editorial response to the Prince Edward County students' actions, he warned white Richmonders to open their eyes to the reality that forcible change might be coming and to prepare for the inevitable battle. As Kilpatrick wryly noted, representatives for the Prince Edward county students "promise[d] litigation" to gain access to the county's "white high schools." The editorial highlighted the legal struggle of white families in Prince Edward County to keep their schools segregated and the NAACP's strategy to overturn separate but equal educational facilities. Though his editorial brought only a mild response, it revealed two issues for the future public debate in Virginia over desegregation of public schools. First, the editorial showed the role that Kilpatrick himself would play in the ongoing desegregation saga. And in an era when television had not yet achieved its pinnacle of influence, the newspaper's role in galvanizing or polarizing local opinion magnified the editor's position. While editors may be a fickle lot, Kilpatrick's opinion shaped one approach in resisting desegregation for southern segregationists.[7] Second, the responses to Kilpatrick's editorial showed a wide range of views on desegregation. The positions readers staked out revealed a divided mind on the issue.[8]

"School Segregation: A Decision Lies Ahead," exclaimed the editorial headline in the *Richmond News Leader* on the evening of May 7, 1951. Devoting more than two-thirds of the editorial column, the *Richmond News Leader* articulated a thoroughgoing segregationist position toward integrated public education a full three years before the *Brown* decision. "It was only a matter of time, of course," the editorial opined, "before zealous Negro forces dropped their campaign for 'equalization' of public school facilities in the South, and turned openly to the goal they have been seeking all along—abolition of all racial segregation in the public school system."[9] The warning expounded the possible ramifications of this decision by the NAACP to desegregate secondary public schools: white abandonment of the tax-supported schools. Though the editor of the *Richmond News Leader* understood the political ramifications of such an action, he could not help painting the struggle in cruder terms. In a tone that would serve the *Richmond News Leader*'s editorial position well during the five-year battle known as massive resistance, Kilpatrick pointed to the fact that desegregation in public schools ultimately would mean "white and colored boys and girls mingling intimately during the formative years of adolescence." As Jane Dailey has noted concerning the use of miscegenation to create fear among white southerners, the combination of race and teenage sexuality had the ability to hold white readers captive to the devices of this segregationist editor.[10]

In the editorial, Kilpatrick laid the foundation for Virginia's notorious "massive resistance" campaign.[11] In its purest form, politicians threatened to close schools rather than desegregate. By 1959, most segregationists, including Kilpatrick, grudgingly conceded that some form of desegregation would occur. Prince Edward County, however, closed its schools from 1959 to 1964, the only district in the nation to use the tactic for a prolonged period.[12]

The editorial and reader responses were preludes to the diverse and heated responses of white people to *Brown*. In a two-pronged attack against desegregationists, Kilpatrick argued that Virginia should withdraw public funds and open "privately financed" schools. Moreover, he thought the best plan for Virginia would be to allow each county to decide for itself whether to desegregate. In an accommodating tone Kilpatrick conceded that where white people outnumbered black people in significant numbers some desegregation might occur. "In the Ninth District (Southwest Virginia)," he suggested, "where [the] white population outnumbers [the] Negro population by 30 to 1, white parents might prefer to assimilate the few colored pupils into the white school system rather than abandon the support of public funds."[13] However, white citizens in the heavily black populated region of Southside Virginia should rightfully stand against the desegregation of schools, Kilpatrick advised.

The majority of reader responses initially opposed Kilpatrick's stance.[14] Published two days after Kilpatrick's statement, a letter from Howard H. Carwile, who served in the Virginia General Assembly and attempted a gubernatorial run as a Democrat against the Byrd machine's candidate, Lindsay Almond, was representative and attacked Kilpatrick's opinion. Calling the editorial "anathema to logic and a travesty on democracy," Carwile argued that "Negro leaders" were exercising their constitutional rights in asking for redress for the second-class treatment heaped upon them. He claimed there was no difference between secondary school and graduate school where desegregation had already occurred without ensuing chaos. Carwile thought secondary education integration could transpire successfully, as long as editorials like Kilpatrick's did not incite people to take drastic steps. In a prescient closing sentence, he wrote: "The path which you advocate is one of anarchy and ruthless retrogression."[15] Carwile's response focused primarily on what he perceived as Kilpatrick's flawed logic concerning democratic forms of justice. In his response, Carwile placed his opposition to Kilpatrick in the context of a universal sense of justice, without invoking a reference to God or divine law.

Two letter writers, however, did comment on the religious and moral dimension in the coming conflict over desegregation, showing the difficulty of using religiously based ideas in public debate and calling attention to the existence of a variety of religiously based views. Asserting there was a difference between secondary and graduate school education, J. A. Moore called the step to integrate graduate education "a stage in the education of the whites in interrace [*sic*] relations," but one that did not need to be turned on its head overnight. "There is hope," Moore thought, "that whites will gradually realize that the common Creator of the two races did not discriminate as He made them different from each other." Noting that legislation would not change the "segregation man[s]" heart, he wrote, the segregationist "is convinced to the depth of his soul that his attitude is as Christian and as patriotic as it can be."[16] Though it was not clear whether Moore himself was a segregationist, he argued for a more gradual approach to desegregation. He believed that over time some white people would come to see that God's design did not involve segregation.

Frances A. Lewis, by contrast, was less conciliatory. In a defiant letter published on May 14, Lewis sarcastically noted that Kilpatrick was correct and Virginia should close its schools because white leaders created fear rather than understanding. "Editorials such as yours," she wrote, "deny that Virginians are decent human beings, capable of understanding just what human dignity is." With one sternly worded question, she outlined the divide over religious engagement with politics and the growing distance among white religious Richmonders concerning desegregation. "How long," Lewis asked, "will you continue to corrupt this generation of readers by inculcating the principles of man-made moralities, tailored to fit a condition of society that is blasphemous and conscienceless?"[17]

Both Moore and Lewis believed in the God-given value of human beings regardless of color. They, however, disagreed about how much external pressure should be placed on white people to embrace desegregation. Moore believed change only came from within—a sort of divine intervention—and that legislation could not help. Using the language of "stages," he affirmed the notion that white people would someday understand their common destiny with black people. Lewis, however, thought that legislation to correct a moral wrong was an appropriate action. She argued that moral claims superseded societal norms and anything less was "blasphemous." In Lewis's opinion Kilpatrick had lost all of his moral currency by defending a "man-made" system as if it were a God-designed commandment. In the years that followed this brief exchange over events in Farmville, the divide grew more pronounced. Moore and Lewis showed how public engagement of religious ideas on political issues created contested boundaries about the relation between religion and public life. The struggle over religious meaning in the desegregation era anticipated the ongoing controversy over the acceptable role of religion in politics throughout the latter half of the twentieth century.[18]

These two responses to Kilpatrick's 1951 editorial reveal how similar theological starting points did not necessarily lead to the same political conclusion. J. A. Moore's call for a cautious optimism about improved race relations highlighted the pietistic notion of internal change by claiming that individuals could change through God's revelation without requiring a reconfiguration of southern social mores. Though segregationist theologies like those created by Sam Bowers existed, Moore did not appear to inhabit a world that endorsed that understanding of racial purity. He envisioned a world where race would no longer matter—something strict segregationists would not have considered. Moore, however, also thought that legal intervention would fail to achieve his more perfect vision of God's kingdom. Frances Lewis, on the other hand, argued that segregation laws were "man-made" and conditional. Using the language of ethics rather than God-talk, she rejected what she saw as the South's perverse worship of segregation. Lewis asserted not only that segregation had outlived its usefulness (if it ever had any) but also that that the courts' intervention would be the only way for white southerners to see the immorality of their way of life.

Almost one year after this mild public debate over possible desegregation ran its course, the desegregation cases made their way to the US Supreme Court. Kilpatrick and Virginia segregationists were pleased with one aspect of the Virginia Supreme Court ruling against the NAACP's challenge to Prince Edward County schools. In a scathing opinion by Virginia's highest court, the state justices had found that the conditions in Prince Edward were grossly "unequal," but claimed they had no precedent to reverse the "separate but equal" doctrine found in *Plessy v. Ferguson*, which was the NAACP's main target with these court cases.[19] In *Plessy*, which created the separate but equal doctrine, the US Supreme Court held that as long as equal facilities existed in public transportation for people of color then the carrier's constitutional obligation was fulfilled. While *Plessy* focused on the narrow issue of transportation, the doctrine had been construed to ordain the South's Jim Crow system but the US Supreme Court used the same legal argument to strip black people of the right to vote in Mississippi in 1898.[20] Some fifty years later, the Virginia justices ordered Prince Edward to rectify the "unequal" situation, but ruled against the plaintiffs by not dismantling the "separate but equal" doctrine found in *Plessy*.[21] In that way, the NAACP's strategy succeeded because it had created conflicting opinions at the state level. The US Supreme Court would have to enter the legal fray to render a more uniform judgment about separate but equal education.

Court-Ordered Desegregation and White Religious Responses

The US Supreme Court brought five of the NAACP's ten cases against segregated public education, including *Dorothy Davis et al. v. Prince Edward County School Board*, to be argued before its bench with the sole purpose of addressing the "separate but equal" doctrine set forth in *Plessy*. Arguments in all five cases were heard before the bench from December 9 to December 11, 1952. The court asked the lawyers to reargue their cases later in spring 1953 for the sole objective of understanding the nature of public education in mid-1860s and the circumstances behind Congress's passing of the Fourteenth Amendment.[22] On the morning of May 17, 1954, the day Myrdal was supposed to be in Richmond, Chief Justice Earl Warren read and promulgated the now famous *Brown* decision to a packed court and with it brought the United States' endorsement of separate but equal in public education to a close. Though the court limited its opinion to public schools, black lawyers and white newspaper editors understood the larger social implications of overturning anything connected to *Plessy*.

From the beginning, the NAACP lawyers representing the "respondents" in the school desegregation cases argued "separate" made African Americans "inferior."[23] As Chief Justice Warren wrote, "The plaintiffs contend that segregated public schools are not 'equal' and cannot be made 'equal,' and that hence they are deprived of the equal protection of the laws."[24] The connection between unequal treatment before the law and lack of redress was an important legal battle for the NAACP to win. To have the case heard by the US Supreme Court and win, the lawyers needed to convince the court that states had violated the intended purpose of the equal protection clause of the Fourteenth Amendment. NAACP lawyers had argued that separate facilities failed to provide adequate educational opportunity, and therefore, equal protection under the law for a number of years. The lower courts, however, had refused to address the *Plessy* doctrine, as noted in the Virginia's Supreme Court's decision to apply *Plessy* rather than confront the inequality of separateness between the races. Chief Justice Warren struck a decisive blow against the southern states when he wrote: "Our decision, therefore, cannot turn on merely a comparison of these tangible factors (equal facilities) in the Negro and white schools involved in each of the cases." "We must," he continued, "look instead to the effect of segregation itself on public education."[25]

The court no longer cared whether a state provided equal facilities and programming—the basis for most legal action taken by the NAACP from the 1920s through the 1940s; it wanted to know the psychological effects of segregation on African American children. Pointing to studies by Kenneth Clark and Gunnar Myrdal among others, the court concluded that at the time of *Plessy* modern psychology had not developed enough to help the court understand the intellectual and emotional consequences of keeping citizens of certain races separated. In stark terms Warren penned, "Any language in *Plessy v. Ferguson* contrary to this finding is rejected."[26] The doctrine of "separate but equal" crumbled under the enormous weight of evidence that "separate" had created a notion of African Americans as "inferior."

As a sign that some white southerners might have been ready to rid themselves of the arcane Jim Crow system while the justices were considering the *Brown* cases, several religious organizations both at the state level in Virginia and at the national denominational level either made pronouncements against segregated public schools or began committee work to draft statements condemning the practice. These statements were for public consumption because no Christian organization filed an *amicus curiae* ("friend of the court") brief related to *Brown*.[27] The Virginia Council of Churches (VCC) acted first. The Virginia affiliate of the National Council of Churches, headquartered in Richmond, established an ecumenical organization for member churches to participate across denominational lines in various activities, including issues of social justice. In the spring of 1954, the VCC announced that separate educational facilities created a serious setback in race relations. In a telling commentary on how a number of white Protestant Christians confessed their complicity in reinforcing an inferior status of black people, the council pointed out "the tardiness of the Christian community in forthrightly dealing with [segregation]." The VCC "urged" members to prayer and study of the situation "in the spirit of boundless, courageous, intelligent good will—which is the spirit of Jesus Christ." The council added: "When the Supreme Court of the United States shall have expressed itself on the matter, we call upon our brothers to receive its expression peacefully and in good faith."[28] The VCC encouraged its member churches to lead the way in positive race relations by acknowledging their failure up to that point. This move was a confession and a call toward active church participation in desegregation but had little direct effect on churches because the statement did not require its constituents to deal with desegregation in any prescribed way. The ecumenical nature of the organization allowed member churches to engage in the conversation—whatever that might be—without forfeiting their identity. The mechanism that created space for public stands on social issues like race relations also limited the result. The public nature of the statement, however, put member churches on notice that desegregation—if the court so chose—should be met with "the spirit of Jesus Christ." A church could disagree with the court's ruling, but it should not interfere with the implementation of the decision.

Denominational pronouncements presented a tougher challenge. The General Assembly of the PCUS addressed the issue of desegregation "innocuous[ly]" when it adopted the following statement at its meeting in 1953: "That the Church practice no discrimination."[29] At the meeting however, a minister from Radford, Virginia, offered an amended recommendation calling for an end to segregation in Presbyterian colleges, presbyteries, synods, and local churches. The assembly voted to "refer" the entire resolution and amendment to its Council of Christian Relations. The referral appeared to be a move to protect the adopted resolution and encourage desegregation in every facet of southern Presbyterianism.[30] The council's position on segregation had been staked out several years earlier. John H. Marion Jr., director of the committee, had openly chastised the PCUS representatives to the Federal Council of Churches concerning their refusal to sign on to a "friend of the court" brief filed with the US Supreme Court supporting the case of Herman Sweatt against the University of Texas law school, one of the NAACP's graduate school cases. Marion responded to the PCUS representatives' decision to abstain from the brief in the *Presbyterian Outlook* by writing: "Can such a system [segregation] be Christian? I tried for a long time to think it wasn't so unchristian, but I've quit trying. I am now convinced that, no matter how fine and Christian individual white people seek to be within the confines of segregation, the pattern itself will stand as a grievous affront to human personality."[31] In his history of southern Presbyterians, E. T. Thompson argues that the Council of Christian Relations at the General Assembly took the referral as an occasion to address the southern Presbyterian church's response to segregation and to encourage the denomination to advance desegregation within the body.[32] Marion's published position suggested that there were leaders in the PCUS who wanted to desegregate denominational institutions, but then when it moved to a wider vote at the General Assembly there was an unease with that kind of complete desegregation.

Late in April 1954, Marion's committee released its report and recommendations to the press. The *Presbyterian Outlook*, published in Richmond but covering Presbyterian life in the South, highlighted the Council on Christian Relation's report which would be presented to the 93rd General Assembly of the PCUS meeting later that May. The report recommended that "enforced" segregation in the General Assembly bodies and institutions (i.e., presbyteries, synods, local churches, and colleges) be rejected. The first recommendation read: "That the General Assembly affirm that enforced segregation of the races is discrimination which is out of harmony with Christian theology and ethics and that the church, in its relationship to cultural patterns, should lead rather than follow."[33] The remainder of the recommendation urged nondiscrimination policies at Presbyterian colleges, retreat centers like Montreat in North Carolina, synods, and presbyteries. It also encouraged local churches to refrain from segregation in its membership. Though contested, the General Assembly, meeting at Montreat, passed the recommendation by a 239 to 169 vote.[34] The southern Presbyterians' statement would be the first of several positive pronouncements by southern white Protestant denominations concerning desegregation of schools.[35] While the pronouncements suggest openness by white Christians to desegregation of church life, the divided vote revealed the nature of the deep divisions within religious communities concerning desegregation. Desegregation of schools, though difficult and trying for many African Americans, would be far easier than desegregating southern life. As J. A. Moore noted in his response to Kilpatrick in 1951 it is easier to change a law than the spirit of someone's heart.

Kilpatrick Responds to *Brown*

White southern politicians initially responded to *Brown* with caution. As one chronicler of Virginia history noted, responses appeared "loyal and constructive" to the court's opinion with the exception of a "critical statement" from Senator Harry F. Byrd Sr.[36] Even James Kilpatrick's editorial on May 18, the day after the decision, sounded more restrained in tone than one would have expected from a man who three years earlier believed a day of tribulation was approaching. Under the title "The Decision," he pointed out that the court had left the door open for the possibility of a slow transition, which it indeed had by deferring implementation arguments until the following October. Kilpatrick urged his readers to remain calm. "It would be sheer folly in this newspaper's view," he wrote, "for the States to summon their legislatures into special sessions. It would be [a] serious error to begin panic-stricken steps toward abolishing all public education."[37]

Though a year later Kilpatrick would unleash a series of vitriolic editorials condemning the US Supreme Court, the May 18 editorial offered a number of positive assertions counterweighted with select warnings. "This is," he suggested, "no time for rebellion. It is no time for a weak surrender either. It is a time to sit tight, to think, to unite in a proposal that would win the Supreme Court's approval. It is time, if you like, for prayer." Kilpatrick thought the "final decree" should take into account several factors, chief among them the white South's right to set the terms for desegregation: "First, the court's final 'ground rules' should be capable of being enforced, as well as men can predict these things, with peaceful acceptance. Second, the rules should be calculated to encourage the southern states in preserving public education. Third, the rules should leave to the States and to the localities the widest possible discretion, consistent with the court's basic opinion, in administering their own affairs according to local conditions."[38] Beating the familiar drum of "states' rights," Kilpatrick deftly sidestepped the decision's more contentious reality—desegregated schools—by explaining southerners' willingness to follow the law of the land as long as the justices realized the gravity of their order. He wrote: "We accept the Supreme Court's ruling. We do not accept it willingly, or cheerfully or philosophically. We accept it because we have to, and we accept it in the profound and prayerful hope that the court, when it comes to writing a final decree many months from now; will exercise wisdom and forebearance [*sic*] in drafting a mandate that will preserve good race relations, encouraging continued public education, and recognize that the States and localities should be left a wide area for local responsibility consistent with the court's opinion."[39] The court's delayed implementation ruling the following year bought some time for segregationists to accept the blow and then reentrench themselves.

As Kilpatrick noted, the US Supreme Court had placed southern cultural institutions in an uncomfortable position. *Brown* created a problem for what many white southerners characterized as their "way of life." Segregationists no longer had national law to protect their idiosyncratic form of race relations and they tried to bring order to what they perceived as chaos. Shortly after the decision public debate centered on the constitutionality of the court's ruling with Kilpatrick leading the way. In what would become a key move, Kilpatrick and others in the "constitutional" camp publicly tried to hold the debate to the merits of the US Supreme Court's constitutional authority to desegregate southern schools without the consent of the individual states (Kilpatrick used the term "constitutional" to distinguish his argument from what he considered lower forms of resistance). He admitted privately that if the court of public opinion had to wade through the moral quagmire of southern racial customs, segregationists were doomed. Corresponding with a doctor in North Carolina over the importance of the constitutional question, Kilpatrick argued: "On the contrary, it seems to me that the South would have some hope, through advancing the idea of interposition, of getting its problem above the sometimes sordid level of race and segregation, and putting it on a high ground of fundamental principles instead."[40] And yet, the very fact that the NAACP targeted public schools meant they understood the importance of attacking a cultural institution. With that assault came the inevitable moral debate.

Richmond Religious Editors and *Brown*

Religious editorial responses to *Brown* in Richmond were varied and revealed the many levels religious engagement with desegregation would take. By 1954, five religious periodicals were published in Richmond. Of the five, only one had a black publisher and black audience, which was Baptist. The other four represented white churchgoers in their respective denominations: Virginia Catholics, southern Presbyterians, Virginia Baptists, and Virginia Methodists. In the case of the Catholics, Baptists (both black and white), and Methodists, the editors wrote to state denominational audiences.

The Presbyterian editor, however, reached a regional audience as an independent paper. The editorial positions ranged along the growing political divide and according to their publishers' positions on race in the American South. The editors' essays mark distinct points on the continuum of religious responses to *Brown*.

Aubrey N. Brown Jr. and the *Presbyterian Outlook*

The US Supreme Court's promulgation of the school desegregation cases coincided for southern Presbyterians with the exact moment they were to debate reunion with the Presbyterian Church, USA (North) and the United Presbyterian Church. On the date of the court's reading of the *Brown* decision, Aubrey Brown, editor of the *Presbyterian Outlook*, editorialized about the Council on Christian Relations' report released two weeks earlier. The second of two editorials—the first covered church union—focused on the thoroughness of the report. In a tone that would later earn him praise for his liberal political candor, Brown continued to speak with remarkable clarity on desegregation within the southern Presbyterian Church. "We can be proud," he wrote about the council's report calling for desegregation of Presbyterian institutions, "of the Assembly's Council on Christian Relations. Its forthright statement condemning racial segregation (*Presbyterian Outlook*, May 3) in all those situations where the church has any relationship to it is something new for a Southern church. It is clear and specific. It cannot be misunderstood."[41] By highlighting the "theology" and "ethics" of the report, Brown indicated that his concern for Christians, particularly Presbyterians, involved how they understood the call of the gospel in their lives. For him the gospel unequivocally called for social engagement. "This pioneering statement," Brown argued, "confronts us with the demand, which none can deny, that the Christian church is to dominate and not be dominated by its culture."[42] Echoing a refrain that guided his editorial positions and active church life, Brown articulated an understanding that the gospel is relevant to all aspects of life for Christians. He held the most prophetic position on the religious continuum of the white religious editors, but framed the position less in overt political liberalism and more in terms of the Hebrew prophets' emphasis on God's justice.

In the May 31 issue of the *Presbyterian Outlook*, Brown addressed the US Supreme Court's decision. Whether he failed to address the matter before this date due to editorial publishing cycles or the *Presbyterian Outlook*'s interest in the Presbyterian Church's reunion question is unclear. Whatever the reason, Brown felt strongly that the court had made the correct judgment. As the *Presbyterian Outlook*'s May 31 editorial declared, "After all, if the Supreme Court of our nation says that segregation is inimical to the fullest development of the character of the children of our schools, we are going to look less than astute or Christian if we try to say something weaker. The law, we say is on a lower level; the gospel is on a higher plain [*sic*]." Affirming his belief that the gospel could transform, and admitting the church's reluctant attitude toward societal transformation, he added: "Let us see, then, if we can make our witness on the higher plain which we claim and for nobler reasons than the pressure of the courts of men. Just now, it would seem, we are a bit behind."[43] For Brown, segregation posed both a moral and political problem.

John J. Daly and the *Catholic Virginian*

On May 14, 1954, the *Catholic Virginian* ran a front-page story covering Bishop Peter L. Ireton's address to the First Friday Club where he talked about desegregated Catholic education. Regardless of the US Supreme Court's upcoming decision, the bishop of Richmond told the group, Catholic schools in Richmond and Norfolk would open their doors to "Negroes." Since the black Catholic high school in Richmond had closed its doors three years earlier and black Catholic parents had to provide Catholic education for their children, the diocese would move to make enrollment at the Catholic schools in the diocese open to all Catholics regardless of race. "Consequently," Ireton said, "we Catholics have the obligation of attempting to provide a Catholic education for them in the Catholic high schools of Richmond."[44]

John J. Daly, editor of the *Catholic Virginian*, responded to the bishop's speech in a brief editorial that declared segregation to be a "moral and religious" issue. "It is only fitting," Daly suggested, "that the [Catholic] Church should have taken a leading role in advocating integration in education, for segregation is a moral and religious problem rather than a political or economic issue."[45] Like Aubrey Brown, Daly argued that Christian conviction about brotherhood meant seeing segregation as opposed to God's will. The church, in his opinion, should lead and not follow on this issue. Daly and the Diocese of Richmond, however, had to deal with a totally separate issue from Protestants and their public schools. The Catholic Church had struggled for many years with how to minister to African Americans. Though Protestants could relegate their actions to Race Relation Sundays because of the segregated nature of denominational life, the Catholic Church faced an internal dilemma: black Catholic parishes with white priests. By the mid-1950s, the Diocese of Richmond had five black parishes. While the Catholic Church could provide a marked difference from the segregated Protestant denominations, it could not remove itself from the racial construction within denominations. The hierarchy continually disagreed over the role that black people could and should play in Catholic leadership.[46] In Richmond, like elsewhere in the South, Catholic "integration" meant black members giving up control of parishes and schools to join white Catholics. These conflicted impulses—ministry outreach to black people and institutional restraint concerning black priests—found expression in Richmond with the opening of five black parishes but the closing of the only black Catholic high school, Van de Vyer, in 1950.[47]

Bishop Ireton's announcement the week prior to *Brown* signaled a shift among some in the American hierarchy that segregated Catholic education would end. In a series of proclamations by bishops in border and upper-South states, culturally mandated segregation in Catholic churches and schools came to an abrupt end. Ireton's statement and Daly's publication of the change was newsworthy because it occurred prior to the US Supreme Court decision, not because it created an open atmosphere toward Catholic desegregation. Even if the Church took the lead in desegregating its schools, as Daly thought, Ireton was responding to a pressing Catholic problem, not a racial one: there was no high school for black Catholics in Richmond. Though the *Catholic Virginian* indicated in 1954 that Van de Vyrer shut down due to low student enrollment, figures supplied by the same paper in 1949 showed 75 students attended the school.[48] More important, 1949 was the first year that all grade levels—first through twelfth—had students. Rather than a school in decline, Van de Vyrer looked like an important piece in the outreach of the Catholic Church to black Richmonders. When the school closed, black Catholics lost a source of pride and educational opportunity.

In July 1954, the diocese announced through its superintendent of schools, Monsignor J. Louis Flaherty, that schools in Roanoke and three Northern Virginia communities would desegregate at the same time. On September 7, eleven "Negro" students enrolled at three Catholic high schools in Richmond.[49] Though the reasons for desegregating Catholic schools may appear less "progressive" in light of the unusual closing of the only black Catholic high school four years earlier, desegregation at the secondary school level occurred in Richmond for the first time in the twentieth century in parochial Catholic schools. Bishop Ireton may have been righting a wrong when in May 1954 he declared that diocesan high schools in Richmond and Norfolk would open on a desegregated basis the following fall, but the decree revealed the messy ramifications of desegregation for black Catholics. It also served as an example of how desegregation, when it occurred in public schools, often erased black institutions in place of white institutional identity.

William L. Ransome and the *Baptist Herald*

The lone black religious editor in Richmond, Rev. William Lee Ransome, covered black Baptist life in Virginia for the Baptist General Association of Virginia and Allied Bodies. Ransome, pastor of First Baptist Church, South Richmond, edited the monthly circular the *Baptist Herald*. His position among the four white editors sheds light on how black religious responses could not separate the legal demands of desegregation from the moral implications of the court's ruling. The different responses by the white and black religious newspapers underscored the tensions concerning desegregation within the wider community.

On the cover of the May 1954 issue of the *Baptist Herald*, the caption above a picture of Chief Justice Earl Warren read: "Hands Down Epochal Decision." Ransome declared that the US Supreme Court decision sounded the death knell for educational segregation. In his editorial, he praised the decision and warned that failure to comply would lead to greater problems for white people. Noting that the attorney general of Virginia had signaled that Virginia might attempt to circumvent the order, Ransome complained: "This is impossible." He reminded his readers that the Racial Integrity laws of the early twentieth century in Richmond, which "designated neighborhoods as either white or black (based on existing racial composition) and prohibited occupancy by new residents of the opposite race," had met a similar fate as educational segregation by the same court in 1917.[50] Although the US Supreme Court declared Richmond's zoning laws unconstitutional in *Buchanan v. Warley*, racial zoning continued through "covenant" agreements attached to closing contracts on homes in the Richmond area.[51] The US Supreme Court, Ransome wrote, "outlawed the racial integrity law on the ground that one cannot do by indirection that which he is forbidden to do directly."[52] Experience informed him that white people would try to do something similar to the *Brown* decision.

Sensing what would become the chosen mode of massive resistance advocates to bypass the court order, Ransome warned against establishing white private schools. He directed his most visceral complaint at white religious people. "Some threaten," he warned, "to seek 'church schools' to do the work of the public schools. It is said that church schools will lend themselves as a haven for those who wish to perpetuate segregation of the races. Church schools should have no segregation." Ransome voiced a common concern among black citizens during this period when he wrote: "The failure of the church made necessary the appeal to the courts. The church can point to little or nothing that she has done in this country to foster the practice of brotherhood which she has so long preached. Every step of social progress for the Negro has been made possible by the United States Supreme Court."[53] The statement was intended as a generalization, and Ransome indicated that he believed that there were "many just-minded white people" in the South. As Ransome remarked in his editorial, newspaper accounts were reporting that the moderator at the General Assembly of southern Presbyterians had said at a recent meeting that the US Supreme Court decision was "necessary, wise and right." Though he pointed to this statement as an example of progressive white religious thinking, Ransome continued to believe the "white" church harmed "Negro" progress more than it helped. "There are other white people," he offered, "who also think that way and who have thought that way, but because of social pressure from their group they have remained silent and inactive. The church is being led into righteousness by the court, and not the court by the church."

Believing the court had rectified a grievous wrong, many black Baptist leaders in Richmond hoped that by remaining calm and dignified, black citizens could show fellow white citizens that what they wanted was equal opportunity.[54] "The average Negro," Ransome claimed, "is not concerned about going to school with white people or anywhere else, but segregation is a badge of inferiority pinned upon the lapel of the Negro's garment. What he wants is the same recognition and privileges accorded all other citizens."[55] Ransome saw in the court's opinion a redress for justice and a means to equal opportunity. While the white editors commented on the radical change caused by the decision, the black Baptist editor voiced the hope of opportunity and pointed an accusing finger at white churches for failing to see that need.

Reuben E. Alley and the *Religious Herald*

Reuben E. Alley, editor of the *Religious Herald* (white Baptist), waited almost two weeks to respond to the court's decision. Publication deadlines and the upcoming annual meeting of the Southern Baptist Convention played a role in the delay. Still, he might have taken a position of cautious waiting. When at last Alley commented on the decision, he showed restraint in praising the court. Calling the decision "inevitable" because of the "improved position" of black people and the United States' place in "international affairs," Alley, unlike Brown, Daly, and Ransome, called the ruling "political, though it carries moral implications."[56] He also asked for the public school system to be spared in any effort to avoid the ruling. Alley then addressed the decision's effect on religious organizations and people.

Though it is not clear that he read W. L. Ransome's editorial in the *Baptist Herald*, Alley responded to critics of Protestant churches who said that the state had taken a greater moral stand than the Church. "The justices of the Supreme Court," he wrote, "make no claim to superior morality. They formulate legal and political opinions to be enforced in this case against the will of the majority. Protestant churches, on the other hand, are motivated by spiritual forces working in the hearts of the members. Every decision by a Protestant church represents the moral attitude of a majority of the group."[57] Pointing to Jesus's teaching to "love thy neighbor as thyself," Alley encouraged readers to "desire the cultivation of divine gifts in others to the same degree that [they] seek for the development of the divine gifts which [they] recognize in [themselves]."[58] The editor remained quiet on the issue for the rest of the summer. Only one editorial mentioned the US Supreme Court decision and that one addressed the negative treatment of Chief Justice Earl Warren by state officials during his visit to Williamsburg in October 1954.[59] Alley, however, devoted space throughout the remainder of 1954 for several sermons and one report by the Virginia General Association of Baptists' Christian Life Commission supporting desegregation.[60]

George S. Reamey and the *Virginia Methodist Advocate*

Under the banner headline "Unsegregated Public Schools," George S. Reamey, editor of the *Virginia Methodist Advocate*, wrote with a cautious, even ominous, tone. "When the United States Supreme Court," he argued, "rendered its unanimous verdict last week on the subject of segregation in the public schools, it passed verdict on one of the most explosive issues before the American people." Claiming that a moderate response to the decision was the best course of action, Reamey staked out his own *via media* between what he viewed as extreme integrationists and segregationists.[61] However, by the late 1950s this middle way turned into open contempt for the court's decision.

The *Virginia Methodist Advocate* editor tipped his segregationist position by noting the court had placed the South in a compromised position. "That there are problems," Reamey claimed, "and serious problems, created by the Court decision goes without saying. Innumerable questions of social adjustment will be called for. Whether for good or ill, a new order in the field of public education in the Southland has dawned." Keeping in mind his audience of churchgoers, he added, "Furthermore, questions raised about non-segregation in the schools may be expected quickly to spread to non-segregation in the churches, hotels, restaurants, residential communities."[62] Reamey was the only editor to point to the tricky proposition of desegregated church membership.

Reamey, as well as others including Kilpatrick, understood that southern social mores rested on a house of cards: removal of a single card could have the whole thing fall in on itself. If segregation could be removed in one arena like education, other arenas were vulnerable, including churches. Separate no longer meant equal, if it ever did. The Methodist editor, like Kilpatrick with his call "to prayer," guided his readers to the place he and they knew best: personal piety. "Christian people," Reamey exhorted, "of whatever creed or race need to be much in prayer to try to find God's will in the whole matter and to seek the kind of guidance which only He can give." Acknowledging that some might misread his position as pie-in-the-sky, he continued, "If this counsel seems to any reader as vague or indefinite, it simply means that we shall have to find the answers to many of our questions as we go along. The important thing is that we start out in the right spirit—in the spirit of Christ—and that we seek above all things to gauge our actions, not by our prejudices or our emotions, but by the will of God." Critics might think Reamey encouraged his readers to ignore the pressing social issue of the day and simply pray. Religious piety, however, did not imply escapism. In the face of the unknown—and in 1954 much about desegregation was unknown—he fell back on a faith that promised God's provision during uncertainty. As a stabilizing force in a person's life, religion can hold the power to give a sense of certainty in an otherwise turbulent era of history.[63] He encouraged his readers to hold on because God would be with them through these pressing events. "Whenever any people," Reamey concluded, "facing a crisis of any kind, take God with them through that crisis, they always come out of it better and stronger for the experience." The problem arises when we interpret God's presence with us during a crisis. Is the believer being challenged to change, like Ransome thought, or is the believer being challenged so that she will remain faithful to the faith, as Reamey thought? Like Alley, he called the decision a major blow against majority opinion. Unlike Alley, however, Reamey attempted to challenge the court's authority. As the years passed his call to piety under the rubric of prayer turned into a call to resistance against the court's order.[64]

Crisis and Engagement

The broad response by the religious editors in Richmond suggests that southern white Christians' deployed multiple frameworks for understanding the *Brown* decision and did so from a variety of circumstances. In this way, they were in conversation with the social norms around them. Some engaged the debate with boldness usually reserved for the category of prophets. Others remained cautious and as such have been labeled as conservative. If Stephen Haynes's model of spectacles of embrace or exclusion can be reappropriated to emphasize the approach of the editor's response to *Brown*, we can see more of a continuum of responses. In this case, rather than seeing exclusion, the priestly function of the church looks to ground the religious community in social and communal traditions. There is a conserving function but it does not have to be politically conservative. Likewise, the prophetic end of the continuum does agitate for change but not always in a politically progressive way. In this frame, the priestly function protects and orders the traditions while the prophetic voice challenges that protection and order, often suggesting that what is protected is the current order instead of an earlier call to an idea like justice. The editors affirmed the importance of God's justice in human endeavors but they differed in what that justice looked like.

Aubrey Brown and William Ransome affirmed the need to see the issues raised in the US Supreme Court ruling as moral and therefore religious. It made little sense to either man that Christians could see anything other than God's hand in the decision. This intimate joining of religious meaning to nonecclesiastical events showed that their initial reactions to *Brown* came from their acute sense of God's purpose in the lives of the oppressed. They believed the church had an interest in the world beyond the church door and *Brown* confirmed that belief. Aubrey Brown thought the court decision opened the door for equal opportunity, but argued that the church must go beyond equal opportunity and welcome African Americans as partners in the work of the kingdom.

As the only African American religious editor in this brief survey, Ransome was hopeful, perhaps more so than Aubrey Brown, that the decision would prompt further change by white Christians. Ransome, however, took that position a step further than Aubrey Brown. As Du Bois argues in *The Souls of Black Folk*, black editors could see the world both as it was and as it should be. Since churches and other organizations that should have advocated the dismantling of Jim Crow laws on moral grounds did not, the court set the injustice straight. Ransome argued that the court intervened with a divine imperative to right a gross wrong. Brown and Ransome both embodied the prophetic impulse in stating their conviction that white churches needed to recommit themselves to the importance of justice in God's kingdom, and that meant desegregation. They did not advocate a politically progressive position, which is how the assertion is understood. In both cases, these men were calling the churches *back* to what they believed was a purer understanding of the gospel message than white Christians' support of southern racial oppression. Not surprisingly, this interpretation of events faced noticeable opposition from religious leaders rejecting desegregation on political grounds.

Reuben Alley and George Reamey both argued that the court overstepped its legal authority. More important to their individual arguments, Alley and Reamey understood the entire crisis from a political perspective, with limited moral implications. *Brown* signaled a shift in constitutional interpretation, they contended; it did not require any response from Christians. This priestly approach caused both men to see radical change as unnecessary and antithetical to the mission of the church or God's vision. The two, however, differed in editorial approach. By advising readers that slow change would have the greatest benefit, Alley argued that change came through the individual because it would allow white people to adapt to the change and see the relative good for relations between the races. His gradualist editorial position focused on the heart of the individual believer. The publication of desegregationist sermons and positive reports of the Christian Life Commission regarding desegregation, however, revealed that the white Baptist editor sensed the changing tide, even if he could not concede the court's decision required a response from the Church. Reamey, on the other hand, argued that federal intervention amounted to a violation of states' rights and that the debate over desegregation could not be extracted from this usurpation of authority. He appeared to move toward the segregationist extreme as the decade dragged on. Reamey held firm to the notion that individuals determine their own moral obligation. The court had made a political decision not a moral one. Even if the court had asserted a constitutional position, it could not meddle in the hearts of Christians.

John Daly spoke on behalf of the bishop in his editorials, a position that, by the time of the *Brown* decision, placed the Diocese of Richmond at odds with the surrounding culture. Daly's position on desegregation helps define the purpose of the continuum. Considering the progressive stance by the bishop, Daly and the *Catholic Virginian* confronted a pressing moral and political issue to advance a prophetic word to Catholic Virginians from the priestly position within church hierarchies. Though the court's decision had no direct effect on the Catholic Church's parochial school system, he wrote clearly about the moral rectitude of the decision. The Catholic editor's main concern involved propagating the announcement of the bishop to the faithful, but by doing so, the editor engaged the political issue of desegregation from a prophetic position, reminding Richmond Catholics of the open nature of the Church. The crisis of desegregation provided a context for engagement. As seen in black diocesan parishes, the Catholic Church in Richmond held no superior position on race. In terms of the continuum, we can see individuals, as well as organizations, expressing their position on a topic without limiting that person or organization to a single theological or political position. More important, the continuum allows for dynamic movement by the individual as new crises arise.

During the course of the crisis, Reamey could hold his segregationist position and at the same time challenge the massive resistance legislature regarding the use of public money for private white schools. Though the shift did not warrant a denunciation of his firm belief that the federal government had intruded where it did not belong, Reamey eventually moved away from segregationists by arguing against the incursion of the state into church matters. He could move away from a rigid ideological position on desegregation when it ran counter to another competing claim (i.e., the separation of church and state) without jeopardizing his commitment to segregation. On the other side of the continuum, Ransome could move to a more moderate position in the 1960s when black student groups challenged the status quo, including his more measured sense of change.[65] The individual does not have to give up his theological or political convictions or fit neatly into a box of society's design.

Brown was only the thunderclap, the presage of things to come for white southerners. The court's decision in 1954 forced white Christians in Richmond to acknowledge the color line. Their reactions to that ruling ran the length of the continuum. The religious editors responded to the immediate crisis and attempted to make theological sense of the possible political change. The religious editors in Richmond voiced positions that would be expressed by regional denominational bodies in the weeks and months following *Brown*. From a vantage point of decades later and through the lens of denominational pronouncements, it appears there were indications that desegregation would occur, even if slowly. The editors' responses, however, suggested that change would be contested at all levels and religious sensibilities did not naturally tend to desegregation. The varying reactions indicate Christianity's ability to engage in public debate without fabricating a single solution. Even when white Christians could produce a clear voice on desegregation, there were substantial social barriers that muted that clarity.

3
ENTERING THE FRAY

White Baptists, Methodists, and Presbyterians in the South convened in the denominational bodies every year between the end of May and July. With the court's ruling, the public pronouncements from those meetings sounded like white Christians in the South were ready to lead the way forward to a desegregated society. At the local level, calls for progress on the issue suggested that even if politicians tried to circumvent the court's ruling calmer heads would prevail. Even as the chorus of conciliatory responses grew from religious organizations throughout the summer of 1954, however, southern politicians began to rattle their sabers, if only rhetorically, in defiance of the court order.[1] Senator Harry F. Byrd Sr. commented on *Brown* from the floor of the US Senate shortly after the decision was delivered. His remarks, along with those of Senator James O. Eastland of Mississippi, called on southern states to defend themselves against the federal incursion into their domain. Byrd called it "a crisis of the first magnitude." The speech appeared innocuous at first, a singular sour note amid a growing sense that desegregation would or should occur. This relative calm led one observer to suggest that white "moderates" believed in the "inevitability of school desegregation." There were networks of concerned groups who wanted to see the desegregation order followed, but as Benjamin Muse noted, those groups assumed an orderly pattern of desegregation would occur and were not in a position to force Governor Thomas Stanley to move faster.[2] Advocates for change sprung to action but the legislative processes, honed by years of Jim Crow politics, worked against their efforts and thwarted their advance. Even if they had pushed for a speedier response, Senator Byrd's political machine held all the power and wasted little time to reveal its intentions to hold on to that power.

On May 19, 1954, Governor Thomas Stanley met former governors John Battle and Colgate Darden, all well-connected lieutenants in Byrd's organization, and issued a formal statement that asserted that Virginia would maintain segregated public schools. "I feel," the *Richmond News Leader* quoted Stanley, "that I should state publicly that, continuing in the next school session of 1954–55, our present school system and policies, including segregation of the races, will be maintained pending final decree of the court in the Virginia case."[3] Governor Stanley also met on May 19 with a white delegation from Virginia's Southside, who, as James Kilpatrick noted in his 1951 editorial, had the most to lose in court-ordered desegregation and who gave Senator Byrd his most ardent support. In the months that followed the court's decision, Virginia's political leaders were securing, at least for the moment, a public racial landscape that resembled every other state of the former Confederacy.[4]

As an example, Georgia's legislature advanced Governor Talmadge's agenda to secure segregated public education. Georgia had a constitutional requirement to provide public education on a segregated basis. Talmadge's plan, and others that followed Georgia's model, kept the public school mandate but allowed localities to divert funds from schools that were required to desegregate to individuals who could then choose segregated educational institutions if they so desired.[5] The plan appeared to be the easiest way around the desegregation order while maintaining the constitutional requirement. White Protestants in the South were uneasy about private school education. Even as segregationist politicians claimed that no public money would be used for parochial education, white Protestant leaders complained that those politicians could not make blanket assurances. The policy also exposed the nature of anti-Catholic sentiment in Protestant circles, but in particular, highlighted why George Reamey balked at the massive resistance plans in Virginia. Public monies could not and should not go to private school education since that would place public tax dollars in the Catholic Church's coffers. The expedient political choice for white segregationists rubbed up against Protestant notions of the separation of church and state.

Had the politicians been paying attention to state and national news organizations for these Protestant denominations, they would have realized that any plan to use public money for private schools would cost them potential allies regarding segregation. Before the *Brown* decision and as an indication that ministers did not always react to political pressures, the Gainesville (GA) Ministerial Association released a statement in March 1954 that stated publicly their determination to keep public school education intact regardless of the court's decision in *Brown*. In language that would appear over and over in the middle part of the decade in ministerial statements, the association declared: "We desire to affirm our faith in continued constitutional government and in the public school system as two of the great cornerstones on which our democracy rests. We are mortally afraid of efforts to tamper with these two cornerstones." The statement added, "We petition our people to be calm and watchful, should leaders seek to hurry them into any action not in keeping with their profession as followers of Jesus Christ. We beg them to stand for the freedom of our public schools from political and sectarian involvement."[6] The Protestant organization's use of "sectarian" language reveals how widespread anti-Catholic sentiment was across the South in the 1950s.

The hard-fought battles over the separation of church and state by sectarians in the eighteenth and nineteenth centuries found expression in the fear that public monies would be used to educate Catholic children in Catholic schools. Protestant periodicals of the era covered every perceived breach in the wall of separation by Catholics and spent as much effort on ridding "popery" influences from government as reporting on *Brown* or desegregation of public schools.[7] Fanned by publications outside the region like *Chris-*

tian Century and inside by the *Virginia Methodist Advocate* and the *Religious Herald*, the anti-Catholic position registered private education as an opportunity for Catholic churches to reap public tax dollars. In Richmond, however, Catholic leaders and laypeople worked hard to keep public schools open for this reason. Even with Catholic leaders advocating support for public schools, or at least not wanting to appear eager for tax money, Protestants worried that would be the result if segregationists' plans to close schools came to pass. Southern politicians had failed to notice this important aspect of American Protestantism's sensibility.

On June 10, Stanley invited governors from the Deep South and border states to a meeting in Richmond to discuss possible responses to *Brown*. The meeting opened with an invocation by Bishop Paul N. Garber of the Virginia Conference of the Methodist Church. Governor Stanley, an active Methodist layman in the Virginia Conference, had asked Garber to lead the assembly in prayer.[8] His presence gave an aura of religious respectability to the proceeding, which the Richmond *Afro-American* did not miss when it quoted Garber praying for the conference to "be loyal to our noble traditions of democracy and religion."[9] Garber's appearance also gave the unambiguous impression that white Christian ministers would again endorse racial oppression. While denominational newspapers informed limited readership and careful readers noticed the nuanced debate within denominations, the Richmond dailies located Christianity's affirmation of segregation in the action of one denominational leader. Even as voices of dissent swirled around the pages of the dailies, Bishop Garber's singular act, and his continued support of segregation, helped shape public opinion about where ministers stood on the question. There was an interesting footnote on the events: the separation of church and state crowd, especially George Reamey, raised no concern about the bishop's presence by the governor's side.

Publicly, except for the *Afro-American*, there was little comment on the apparent endorsement of segregationist culture by this representative of a culturally dominant white denomination.

Within three years of the governors' meeting, however, Richmond's Christian community engaged in a significant public debate over Christianity's purpose within that segregationist culture, often with Garber's own charges in the Methodist church leading the way. Yet the discussion over the role of religious influence mattered little to southern political leaders as the reality of desegregated schools encroached upon southern order. They needed a plan.

As the events of May 17 faded, the hope for a peaceful resolution of the US Supreme Court's decision faded as well. By late June, Stanley issued the most pointed comment about resisting *Brown* when he declared: "I shall use every legal means at my command to continue segregated schools in Virginia."[10] In August 1954, he appointed a thirty-two-person committee called the Virginia Commission on Public Education (VCPE), chaired by state Senator Garland Gray from Virginia's Southside. All the members were white. The Gray Commission, as the body was commonly known, took until November 1955 to issue its findings regarding Virginia's public education system and desegregation.[11] As Kilpatrick had pointed out in his editorial the day after the *Brown* decision had been handed down, the court had given southern states time to react, and their evolving plan moved toward resistance. Between 1954 and 1955, Virginia's political leaders shifted their stance from one of moderation to outright resistance.[12]

As the Gainesville Ministers Association statement indicated, ministers across the South made public pronouncements encouraging leaders to follow the court's lead for desegregated schools. The reports of these statements were brief and often carried little comment. Denominational periodicals might reference the statements in editorials in mostly positive tones, but they were just as likely to emphasize the caution noted in the statements as any outright affirmation of the court's decision.[13] Since the denominational institutions of the South had made similar public statements in the immediate aftermath of the decision, these statements should have surprised no one. What has often been missed in the lull between the court's decision and the segregationist laws that attempted to circumvent that decision is the awareness and engagement of religious folks in the events. Indeed, in Richmond from 1954 to January 1957 both ministers and laypeople formed organizations or used denominational structures already in place to combat massive resistance. Two such organizations, the Virginia Council on Human Relations (VCHR) and the Richmond Ministers' Association (RMA), would play a role in challenging Virginia politicians as they maneuvered to keep schools segregated. John H. Marion would play an important role in both organizations.

The sentiment among Richmond's black and white Christian ministers was for some form of desegregation, a less than resounding note for full integration but a significant position nonetheless. The VCHR, including its Richmond affiliate, and the RMA asserted a counterclaim to the segregationists. Unlike the assessment that there was little value in "going on record," as Myrdal had called it, the ground-level work done by both ministerial and lay leaders in these organizations created an alternative understanding of desegregation in Richmond and indicated they were willing to hold political leaders accountable. The record indicates that some white ministers had abandoned their segregationist brethren, much to the consternation of the latter, but their efforts have received little attention. The networks at the local level showed how theological differences could be set aside to address a perceived moral outrage. Organizations like the VCHR allowed some Catholics and Protestants to work together, even if Catholics did so as individuals and not part of the Church. In the midst of heightened tensions between Catholics and Protestants during the growing Cold War era, Richmond's Catholic presence gave Protestants agitating for a desegregated social order an ally in the fight with southern politicians. The work of organizations like the VCHR shows how individuals in Richmond bridged organizations together to assert a political position in moral form but one not attached to denominational structures. These networks, however, had to work by persuasion instead of political force, and this fact highlighted their greatest strength and its concurrent weakness. The VCHR and RMA could boldly advocate for desegregation and alter the rhetorical center for white citizens in the Jim Crow South. They could not, however, guarantee success through political change.

Gray Commission

As the US Supreme Court heard implementation arguments for *Brown*, Virginia began a steady process to avoid any desegregation orders. The Virginia Commission on Public Education (also known as the Gray Commission) met to draft a proposed legislative agenda concerning public education in Virginia. As the commission worked, two issues became clear. First, Virginia's mandatory educational system required that localities provide suitable public education for its citizens. Disbanding public education would meet stiff opposition from a variety of quarters in the state, as Kilpatrick observed about desegregation in southwest Virginia in the 1951 editorial, so politicians quickly moved to flanking positions. Since Virginia required public education and *Brown* affected public education, Virginia's politicians had to find a way to continue public schools without abiding by the US Supreme Court order. Second, to circumvent the court's order anticipated in *Brown II*, the Commonwealth of Virginia had to find a way to publicly fund "private academies." The Gray Plan made three recommendations: tuition grants for students wishing to attend private schools rather than integrated ones, a pupil assignment plan, and an amendment to compulsory attendance law.[14] On November 11, 1955, the commission sent its recommendation to Governor Stanley, and he set November 30 for the special session of the General Assembly to consider the Gray Plan.[15] Meeting in a special session later in November, the General Assembly would debate the issues raised by the Gray Plan, specifically the need to amend Section 141 of the Virginia constitution, which required "efficient" public education throughout the Commonwealth of Virginia.

Just before the General Assembly considered the Gray Plan, however, Kilpatrick unleashed his harshest criticisms to date of the

Brown decisions in a series of editorials. In so doing, he redirected the debate from limited compliance to outright resistance, and in the process changed the tone of his editorial position from one of limited desegregation to "nullification" of the court's ruling. As the opening editorial, "Transcendent Issue, II," explained, the Gray Commission had pointed to a more vexing problem than integrated schools: judicial legislation. "If the commission correctly states the degeneracy of constitutional process," Kilpatrick argued, "does not Virginia have a right and a duty to interpose its sovereignty in a valiant effort to halt the evil?" He vowed to articulate fully both Virginia's historical place in constitutional history and a state's right to *interpose* its will against the Union.[16] On the following day, Kilpatrick began to expound on a long-forgotten legal argument in English common law, but one raised by defenders of a state's right to slavery, and gave intellectual credence to what later became known as "massive resistance."[17] In a move of questionable motive, Kilpatrick wanted to get the discussion off racial inferiority an argument he feared the segregationists would lose, and onto the issue of constitutional authority, what he called the "high ground of fundamental principles," which was a noticeably different "higher plane" than that presented by Aubrey Brown or John Marion.[18] Virginia had the right, inherent in the US Constitution, Kilpatrick argued, to interpose its will over Congress—or, in this case, the US Supreme Court— if the state believed that the federal government had overstepped its authority. While the Gray Commission had been charged to find a practical way around the court order, it did not deal directly with whether the court's action was "legal," but it raised that possibility as an issue. Kilpatrick had his opening. Publishing the Virginia and Kentucky resolutions that decried the passing of the Alien and Sedition Acts of 1798 on the editorial page of the *Richmond News Leader*, Kilpatrick and the *Richmond News Leader* equated the congressional action to increase the powers of the federal government in 1798 to the US Supreme Court's decision in *Brown*. Virginia's response in 1798, he argued, was to assert state sovereignty over federal regulation, even when it never invoked the statute. This interpretative leap allowed Virginia the "right of interposition" against a wayward US Supreme Court concerning desegregation.[19]

The interposition argument gained ground following Kilpatrick's publications. By his own admission, Kilpatrick did not anticipate the enthusiasm for interposition his statements would engender. Writing in an almost giddy tone to Byrd, he stated: "This interposition movement is snowballing so fast I can scarcely keep up with the hour-by-hour developments." Intentional or not, while trying to support the work of the Gray Commission, he began to undermine it. He wanted Byrd to know the importance of the Gray Plan to him. "I am anxious to get the movement rolling ahead here in Virginia," he wrote, "and yet I do not want to jeopardize the Gray Commission's referendum in January. There must be some way, however, that we can create a little news on it here without affecting the referendum in any way."[20] Whether Kilpatrick meant to "derail" the Gray Plan remained unclear. The fervor over interposition, however, shifted the discussion away from possible forms of compromise on desegregation inherent in the Gray Plan, like local option, to outright resistance to the court's order. By the end of the special session of the General Assembly in November, Senator Byrd's organization began to assess its position. Nothing could, or should, be done to interfere with the referendum set for January 1956 asking voters their opinion on altering the state constitution's public education section.[21] Segregationists in Virginia, however, saw an opportunity in interposition not present in the Gray Plan: total resistance.

Challenging Massive Resistance: VCHR, Religious Editors, and the Gray Commission

As ministers like John Marion had made clear during the late 1940s and into the 1950s, white Christian leaders as a whole no longer gave credibility to a segregated order, though they differed in their approach to reach this goal. Marion's declaration that segregation was a sin in 1953 put political leaders on notice. The host of public pronouncements from denominational bodies across the region suggested that some leaders were ready for change. These signals should have reminded segregationists that to move against slow, steady desegregation of schools would have caused pushback from ministerial ranks since they had already framed the issue in moral rather than political terms. Ministers, however, understood that not all within their ranks or their congregations were in the same place. Often, as the formation of the RMA makes clear, ministers had to reach across denominational boundaries to find kindred spirits. The formation of the Southern Regional Council (SRC) emphasized another way religious leaders could band together for change. Individuals who aligned with these organizations showed a willingness to work outside religious bodies altogether to bring about social reform of the region. The state affiliate Virginia Council on Human Relations (VCHR) worked to bring about desegregation. The body chose a desegregation crusader to run the group.

Two years after the RMA's formation, VCHR organized (1955) when a group of twenty-some "white and Negro leaders, representing the Protestant, Roman Catholic and Jewish faiths" met at the Central YMCA in Richmond. This group served as a catalyst for social engagement in Virginia throughout the 1950s and 1960s. A number of individuals active in the RMA also participated in the VCHR, including its new executive director, John Marion. In describing the new organization, Rev. W. Carroll Brooke, an Episcopal priest from Staunton and the first president of the council, noted that its purpose was educational, similar in intent to the SRC. By promoting "greater unity in the South" and addressing "race tension, racial misunderstanding and racial distrust," the group believed that it could overcome the differences between the races. However, and on this Brooke was emphatic, the VCHR would not be involved "in any political activity."[22] The VCHR's relationship to the SRC provided the primary reasoning behind its seemingly apolitical position. The early money to sponsor the group came directly from the Ford Foundation's Fund for the Republic through the SRC. The SRC guarded its tax-exempt status by discouraging affiliates from participating in political activity.[23] While the public statement made clear the nonpolitical emphasis of the group, its creation amidst the chaotic years of the desegregation controversy and as a response to the formation of the Defenders of Liberty and State Sovereignty suggested a different course.[24] The group's work, however, would emphasize persuasion.

In its first action, the group chose John Marion as its first executive director. The fiery preacher and advocate of a desegregated South left little doubt that the organization's apolitical stance would be tested. Marion proved a wise pick on multiple levels. Although he might have ruffled some feathers, his outspoken nature roused numerous "liberals" on racial issues to join the battle.[25] He also worked tirelessly in Richmond to educate groups about why desegregation helped all citizens. Under his leadership, which lasted until mid-1958, the VCHR grew to nearly 1,500 members and established a local affiliate in every major city in the state, with Richmond leaders creating a local chapter in 1957 at the height of the standoff in the legislature over desegregation.[26] As the events of 1955 and 1956 unfolded, the RMA, the VCHR, and the Virginia chapter of the National Conference of Christians and Jews (NCCJ) asserted a moral opposition to the growing political resistance to desegregation.

Peter Mellette, director of the NCCJ in Virginia, worked under the radar and advanced an aggressive educational program to help Richmond move on desegregated schools. Taking his official position in January 1955, after moving from St. Louis, Mellette orchestrated a series of meetings with parent teacher association groups in Richmond's white schools. On the evening of January 13, he invited Emerson Smith, head of the VCC; John Marion; and Murray Friedman, head of the Anti-Defamation League in Richmond, to join him in a discussion about how desegregation would work and possible plans for its implementation. Referring to the events several days later in a letter to his supervisor in New York, Mellette noted that educational leaders in Richmond had been asking for help. Richmond school superintendent H. I. Willett served on the board of the Richmond branch of the NCCJ. "Just this past week," Mellette wrote, "I arranged and served on a four-member panel before the largest high school P.T.A. in Richmond. It was a very successful evening and certainly did our conference here no harm."[27] The conversation in the early part of 1955 hinted that a slow and steady change was coming. Mellette's connections to both civic and religious leaders meant he could create venues of discussion that focused on desegregation. Late in 1955, at the height of the Gray Commission's work, he would bring together, under the auspices of the NCCJ, Richmond public school and Catholic diocesan school leaders for a conference titled "Human Relations Problems in Education."[28] While architects of massive resistance built their defense of segregated schools, people like Peter Mellette built coalitions and labored to bring about change, even if that meant slowly and in measured steps. Through the middle part of 1956, these advocates for a desegregated school system believed their aims were achievable. They, however, could not anticipate that the political players themselves were altering the terms of the discussion. As the Gray Commission publicly noted, local option suggested that localities would have control over the decision. In this instance, persuasion could have worked.

With the unveiling of the Gray Plan, the work of the VCHR and Mellette with the NCCJ appeared to be headed in the right direction. Aubrey Brown placed the VCHR's first public statement pertaining to desegregation on the front page of the *Presbyterian Outlook* for the November 14 issue. The council had labored hard to render a position for the upcoming special session of the General Assembly, which would address the recommendations of the Gray Commission. In so doing the VCHR flirted for the first time with its apolitical status by advocating a stance on which the General Assembly should act. The statement, however, placed the recommendations to the state legislature within the broadest sense of democracy. The recommendation stated that many people of Virginia held a deep conviction that the country's reputation and the "essential dignity" of every citizen were "closely bound up with the way we practice our democratic faith."[29]

The VCHR's plan for desegregation placed the onus of responsibility on local school boards and superintendents. The six-point scheme outlined the governor's responsibility to uphold all state and federal laws. It also delineated how local governments should create biracial committees to oversee the best way to implement desegregation, keeping everyone's "various interest" in mind. This important recommendation showed sensitivity to the pressures of desegregation that would not be present when schools finally desegregated years later. Point five specifically encouraged religious groups and the media, perhaps directed at Kilpatrick, and to a lesser extent Virginius Dabney, editor of the *Richmond Times-Dispatch*, to "seek to build in every way possible a climate of understanding in which respect for facts and reverence for law shall be preserved and fostered."[30] In its first public pronouncement, the VCHR, speaking through its executive director, managed to politicize its cause. The council endorsed desegregation and told Virginia leaders how to accomplish the task with a step-by-step plan. The organization also signaled to potential voters that the local option placed control in their hands, which meant the VCHR could still convince voters to agree to desegregation.

Some moderate leaders, however, appeared to acquiesce on the referendum question, and in particular the Gray Plan's tuition grants. The use of public monies for private education rubbed many folks the wrong way and became the focus of debate in the General Assembly special session. The session called for a referendum in early 1956 to vote on the plan. The white religious editors, however, waged a vigorous campaign against the referendum.[31] Although all of the white religious editors urged a "no" vote, none of them used the same argument. Reuben Alley and George Reamey denounced the Gray Plan in the early weeks of December 1955. Both the Baptist and Methodist editors argued that the commission's proposal endorsed the use of public money for sectarian schools. Both editors also claimed that there were few guarantees that public monies would not be used for parochial education. "Neither the Gray Commission nor the General Assembly," Alley warned, "seems to have answered this important question."[32] He could frame the discussion around church–state issues, without arguing for desegregation. As others have pointed out, this form of argument meant that moderates condemned legislative actions without embracing any notion of desegregation.[33] For Alley and others, walking the tightrope between accommodation and conviction created a "dilemma," which enhanced opposition against massive resistance. Reamey was even more pointed against the Gray Plan. "For example," he wrote, "what assurance is there, if any at all, that the term 'private schools' will not quickly be interpreted to include church schools? It is not difficult to envision a situation when, if the law is changed, a vociferous demand will arise that Roman Catholic parochial schools be included in the distribution of tax funds."[34] In both cases, a "no" vote on the referendum ensured a true separation of church and state, making segregation irrelevant.

The racial element, however, could be added to the church–state arguments. Reamey went so far as to claim "we are not prepared to agree that largescale integration **at this time** is the Christian step to take." He applauded the interposition argument and thought the court overstepped its authority and that "current proposals for exercising the 'right of interposition' appear to be well worth investigating."[35] Yet, for Reamey the notion of public monies to operate private schools created a conflict with the "wall of separation." The "yes" or "no" format for the referendum forced Reamey to choose between his segregationist and ecclesiastical sympathies. On this point, Reamey's religious allegiances outweighed his regional sentiments.

Two contemporaries made comments on the editors' statements—one very public and the other private. Kilpatrick editorialized against Reamey's judgment on the impact of tuition grants under the editorial "Objection 6." He dismissed Reamey's argument as unfounded. "It will help perhaps," Kilpatrick argued, "if all those who are concerned about the Gray Commission's program, will keep in mind the purpose for which 'tuition grants' are recommended. This purpose is simply to provide some educational opportunity, equally available to white and colored children, as an alternative to forced integration. Persons who ultimately may be driven to the last resort of tuition grants will have no sectarian interest in common; their mutual desire will have nothing to do with a Protestant or Catholic education."[36]

Kilpatrick never fully understood why Protestant editors and ministers raised this concern regarding public money for private schools. In his reasoned approach to segregation, Kilpatrick allowed for the use of grants for both black and white children to receive an education, if they so chose, within a segregated environment. In so doing, his logical starting point was holding on to segregated "public" schools: parents paid taxes and they should have the right to decide how that money was spent on their children's education. He could not imagine how anyone would understand the Gray plan any other way.

David J. Mays, a Richmond attorney who served as general counsel for the Gray Commission, confided in his diary that Reamey, a fellow classmate at Randolph Macon College, "failed to read the report or at least to grasp it, since his editorial is completely misleading. Rube Alley, another of my RMC classmates, . . . is bitting [*sic*] at us, too."[37] Mays anticipated some type of criticism and convinced the Gray Commission in August 1955 to insert provisions in the amendment that tuition grants would not be used for parochial schools, which may have led to his consternation over the Methodist and Baptist editors' attacks.[38] Though both Alley and Reamey thought the destruction of public education would harm Virginia's school children, specifically white children, both men championed the notion of a white Protestant hegemony articulated through groups like Protestants and Other Americans United for the Separation of Church and State. At least on this issue, the internal debates over desegregation revealed fault lines that would grow as white Protestants began to lose control of that hegemony. The anti-Catholic position of both editors reinforced notions by Protestants in the South that public monies would fund Catholic schools. The level to which church–state watchdogs would go in the first three-quarters of the twentieth century deafened them to Catholic voices who were equally troubled that tax money would be used for private education of any kind.

The racial issues of the 1950s cannot be extracted from the social and religious context of the period. Before the Second Vatican Council, mainline Protestants in the United States waged a constant war against anything that *hinted* of popish intent. Since Kilpatrick thought religion played only a minor role in political affairs and Mays privately felt antagonistic toward religion, they both failed to comprehend the seriousness of the charge by Alley and Reamey that tuition grants posed a religious threat to Virginia Protestants and their control over public education. More important, they lost at least one potential ally over this issue. Both Kilpatrick and Mays thought of themselves as astute readers of history; yet, both men overlooked the long struggle that Baptists and Methodists had overcome to practice their faith in a free society. White Virginia Baptists like Rueben Alley were keenly aware of the persecution of Baptists in Virginia until the creation of the religious liberty statute in the state's constitution during the American Revolution.

By the 1950s, white Protestants in the South, however, were the "state" in the sense that they controlled the cultural disposition of the region. Their aim on the wall of separation shifted from government incursion into church matters to church (read: Catholic) incursions into government matters, like parochial education. In Richmond, however, Richmond Baptists and Methodists spoke a similar language to Richmond Catholics. John J. Daly, editor of the *Catholic Virginian*, carried out his own crusade against the referendum, urging Catholics to perform their civic duty and vote in January. He devoted editorial and news space to both sides, perhaps tipping his hand to the anti-referendum side but remaining fair to each. Pointing to the number of questions the Gray Plan raised rather than answered, Daly urged his readers "to study all available information, and to consider themselves obligated to go to the polls on 9 January and cast a ballot based on right principles."[39] For the time being, he left "right principles" undefined.

On December 23, however, the *Catholic Virginian* reported a statement by the Social Action Committee of the Northern Deanery of the Richmond Council of Catholic Women concerning the upcoming referendum. In the statement, the committee attempted, in the words of the *Catholic Virginian*, "to apply Catholic principles to the practical question of the appropriate Catholic attitude toward the referendum." Asserting the committee's opposition to the referendum, the statement read in part: "Without any doubt an affirmative vote in the referendum in January will be a vote for a more or less permanent system of segregation in schools supported by State funds." The committee argued first that by standards of "natural moral law" segregation denied dignity to people of color because it denied their humanity, and therefore segregationists fell short of divine law. In a strongly worded section, the committee made clear the connection between segregation and sin. "It can hardly be disputed," they wrote, "that strict justice is violated by racial segregation, but even if justice were not violated no one would pretend that charity is not wounded. Racial segregation is certainly **a sin** against charity and, in the Christian dispensation, is certainly immoral." The statement also addressed the tuition grant portion of the proposed amendment. The committee highlighted the major fear of Protestants—that grants would be offered to parochial schools—as a reason to vote against the referendum "lest parents of children attending parochial schools see in the referendum a possibility of relief from a heavy financial burden." "An examination of the wording of the referendum ballot," the statement warned, "will reveal that the State aid proposed by the Gray Commission is limited to nonsectarian schools." The Social Action Committee condemned the referendum in the strongest terms possible.[40]

The committee argued against the referendum, focusing on two points. Theological conviction informed the first line of reasoning. The Social Action Committee stated in clear theological terms that segregation was a "sin." Denying the human dignity of a creature of God profaned not only natural law, which should guide civic law, but was an affront to the dignity of God. The committee thus defined segregation in moral rather than strictly political terms. A vote for the referendum would sustain segregation (read: "sin") and Virginia Catholics should not support such an action. Self-defense accentuated the second point. As the Baptist and Methodist editors pointed out to their own readers, the Social Action Committee's statement claimed that tuition grants sounded like a way to circumvent the separation between church and state over religious instruction. The committee explicitly informed Virginia Catholics that the grants could not go to parochial schools. Ironically, Richmond Catholics understood the effort put forth by David Mays to get the nonsectarian language added to the referendum.

One week later, Daly gave front-page coverage to Adele Clark's message to Catholic women concerning the upcoming referendum. Serving as legislative chairwoman of the Richmond Diocesan Council of Catholic Women, she reminded members that the council voted during the previous summer to do whatever it took to preserve public education. Clark stated she would vote "no" on January 9. The news item followed the publication of a newsletter by Mrs. W. J. Jonak of Portsmouth, Virginia, diocesan council president, to council members. Jonak included Clark's full notice that the referendum, if approved, would end compulsory education in Virginia, and with it, public education.[41] Daly editorialized three days before the referendum, "the only way to vote is to do so on the basis of right principles." This time, however, he recalled the statement of the Social Action Committee of Northern Virginia Deanery Council of Catholic Women and the testimonials of Miss Adele Clark and Mrs. W. J. Jonak.[42] "Right principles" meant a vote against the referendum through Catholic social teaching and moral law. Catholic leaders stated publicly that maintaining segregation of public schools in Virginia would set their community on a dangerous path, and in the process, protected their standing with a Protestant-dominated society. With a touch of irony, many Protestants and Catholics in Richmond were on the same page regarding this issue.

Aubrey Brown had already shown distaste for Catholic-baiting, favoring a forward-gazing vision for a fully desegregated society. In the pages of the *Presbyterian Outlook*, Aubrey Brown derided the Gray Plan and the upcoming referendum for its single-minded sense of destructive purpose for taking money away from public schools. "It appears to be the height of absurdity," the editor wrote, "to believe that the already-low standards of public education of many southern states can be maintained or elevated by any of the presently-proposed plans calling for private schools operated by tuition payments from the public treasury."[43] While several states had considered tuition grants, Brown editorialized against the Gray Plan, without naming it. He argued not from a theological or purely religious perspective; rather he stated that support for two systems of education would mean disaster for the educational opportunities of Virginia's children.

Brown's lack of theological justification for condemning the referendum, however, should not be interpreted as a purely political stance. Of the three white Protestant editors, Brown affirmed integration throughout society, not just in schools. As he made clear in 1957 speech, the forces of desegregation had a moral obligation to advance Christ's cause. Referring to the southern church's potential role in the changing times, Brown said: "Never, it would be safe to say, have more men and women in the South been driven more resolutely to discover the real meaning of the Christian gospel, never have they confronted more starkly the grim, forbidding and corporate nature of sin, never have the claims of the Christian conscience been pressed more demandingly upon them, never have they been challenged more persistently to fulfill the mission of the church of Jesus Christ."[44] Aubrey Brown integrated his Christian faith into a web of progressive social agendas. To speak out against injustice equated with speaking out about the nature of God. When he called the tuition grant plan absurd for taking money from public education to the detriment of both black and white students by siphoning monies from public schools for private schools, he advocated a specific political position. Behind that condemnation laid a prophetic rage against injustice—unequal education—that came from his conviction that God's nature rejects oppression. Brown ended a November 21, 1955 editorial by saying, "In the grandest periods of Christian history, evil men have always been disconcerted by Christian witnesses who refused to be manipulated to support wicked purposes."[45] In the mid-1950s both sides of the ideological spectrum saw themselves championing the Christian witness against "wicked purposes."

The tactic of persuasion by the VCHR and denominational newspapers appeared to fail. When voters went to the polls on January 9, 1956, they voted "yes" nearly 2 to 1 in favor of the referendum, which created the legitimization of a constitutional convention to address the compulsory education laws of Virginia's constitution. The Gray Plan, if approved in the special election, set March 10 for the constitutional convention. Interposition advocates now believed a decisive defeat of *Brown* and reassertion of separate but equal remained possible. Meeting after the vote and just before the constitutional convention, the General Assembly went to work on a series of interposition bills—one having been drafted by Kilpatrick.[46] By the end of the session, the Gray Plan lay gutted on the floor of the state house. Rather than accepting token desegregation as the Gray Plan called for, through local option, which numerous white religious groups would have endorsed, Virginia's political leadership chose the path of massive resistance.[47] Senator Byrd's call in February for "massive resistance" by southern states against the *Brown* decision became the rallying cry for the rest of the South regarding desegregation of public schools.[48]

Governor Thomas Stanley suggested in early August that he would seek legislative support to deny funds to any locality that desegregated its schools. For the first time since the formation of the Gray Commission, the local option was losing ground to tuition grants. Stanley, however, claimed that Virginia would not tolerate any form of school integration, which the local option recommendation left open as a possibility. In superseding its authority over the US Supreme Court, Virginia attempted to place its sovereign rule over local communities that might want some form of desegregation.

The VCHR made its second statement on desegregation of public schools in response to Stanley's threat. In issuing its announcement, the VCHR called on the governor and the General Assembly, which would be meeting in a special session later in August, to consider that Virginia's constitution required "an efficient system of public free schools." They also called on the legislature to consider a local option plan for localities ready to desegregate their schools.

Virginia's attorney general at the time, Lindsay Almond Jr. (who would play a key role in the closing of schools in Virginia two years later as governor), spoke to a state law enforcement conference in Roanoke two days after the VCHR's statement and explained the Byrd organization's opposition to local option. Calling the VCHR an "integrationist" organization, he rejected the executive committee's request, saying it was detrimental to the efficient working of public schools because "mixed schools would isolate [those schools] from community support."[49] In an interesting semantic twist, both sides highlighted the "efficient" system required by law; however, the VCHR interpreted the idea to mean open and perhaps integrated. The Byrd machine understood it to mean closed or segregated. At the end of the special session, Governor Stanley's plan for "no compromise" won out and the VCHR appeared again as a "voice crying in the wilderness."[50]

As Jeffery Hadden noted in his survey of ministers' and congregations' responses to the civil rights movement in the 1960s, the separation between the pulpit and the pew over social issues caused tensions within congregations.[51] These spectacles of exclusion became more pronounced in the 1960s as lay boards and deacon bodies exerted their displeasure with preacher meddling. The early 1950s, however, showed no signs of this rift. Ministers had gained a certain level of public respect by the 1950s, which was connected to Christianity's cultural ascendancy in the Cold War era.[52] Richmond ministers asserted their moral authority when they condemned the political tactics of massive resistance.[53] In the Statement of Conviction by the Richmond Ministers' Association, area ministers challenged the notion that Christianity endorsed continued racial separation. Bishop Garber's presence at the governors' meeting in 1954 suggested southern white Christians supported the continued use of Jim Crow order. The ministers' statement, however, highlighted a growing division among white southern Christians regarding racial politics.

4
GOING ON RECORD

Maintaining the status quo, Virginia's public schools opened in the fall of 1956 on a segregated basis for the third year since *Brown*. The goal set out by Governor Stanley and the segregationist politicians to keep Virginia's schools segregated using any means necessary had come to fruition through the special session of the General Assembly. At least at one level, these politicians had elevated Virginia's position as a leader of white southerners' vision of a segregated society, even in the face of evidence to the larger shifts taking place in American society and notable opposition at home.

In Virginia, four school districts used the massive resistance laws to keep segregation in place. The early concern over the *Brown* decision had found James Kilpatrick open to limited desegregation where African Americans accounted for a small percentage of the population, like areas east of the Blue Ridge Mountains and the entirety of the Shenandoah Valley. Yet by 1957, at least two districts in that part of the state used the massive resistance laws to close their doors. Both Warren County schools and Charlottesville City schools shut down operations during the 1957–1958 school year. These moves might have suggested a tougher response from parts of Virginia that held a larger black population or in some cases a majority population. As Kilpatrick had feared, those areas where black and white Virginians blurred clear lines of separation became the front lines in the battle to end segregation. Given that the US military had begun to desegregate in the late 1940s and that Tidewater Virginia was quickly becoming home to the largest military industrial complex in the world, Norfolk's school board opted to close the district's doors rather than open its schools. In Warren County, Charlottesville, and Norfolk these closures all represented responses to local National Association for the Advancement of Colored People (NAACP) efforts to enroll black students in white public schools. In each case, though the school term was disrupted for a period, the district reopened its doors while keeping the schools segregated. Prince Edward County schools, however, suffered the greatest strain when the school board decided in 1959 to shut all public schools. Prince Edward County, one of the cases that formed *Brown* and that was under the 1955 "all deliberate speed" order in *Brown II*, refused to allow black students to enroll in white schools. From 1959 to 1964, there were no public schools in operation in the county. Virginia was not unique among other southern states attempting to circumvent the court's desegregation order, since all of them and a few of the border states removed local options to open on a desegregated basis. Richmond never closed its schools, though the NAACP did petition on behalf of a student to attend a white-only school in 1958. It was clear by fall 1956 that Virginia politicians would do whatever it took to maintain school segregation.

The spectacle of Little Rock, Arkansas, looms large in the public consciousness of this period. The federalized Arkansas National Guard, followed quickly by the arrival of members of the US Army's 101st Airborne division, hardened battle lines for white southerners as the federal government used military power to ensure the desegregation of Little Rock's Central High School. Since the images of members of the Little Rock community yelling at black students being escorted into the school has such a powerful hold on both the imagination and history, it is little wonder that few studies have been done on work performed by white Christians in the face of segregationist politicians. Sociologists Thomas Pettigrew and Ernest Campbell studied Little Rock and determined "sectarian" voices were the loudest for segregation. Even as their study revealed that Protestant ministers in Little Rock actively encouraged desegregation of the public schools, Pettigrew and Campbell's work still holds significant weight when thinking about white Christians and the days of massive resistance.

The extended interaction by the Richmond Ministers' Association (RMA) and Virginia's political machine in the early months of 1957 reveals how the desegregated ministers' group engaged in the public debate over desegregation, asserted their moral authority, and interpreted both scripture and the US Constitution regarding desegregated public schools. The ministerial ranks had divisions on desegregation but few of those who participated in the RMA stood in the strict segregationists' camp, resembling in many ways what Pettigrew and Campbell found in Little Rock: Richmond's Episcopalian ministers often approved of segregation as much as "sectarian" preachers. The competing claims about God's role in human affairs, however, allows us to understand how ministers engaged the political process. As with other social issues, ministers who supported desegregation were thought to have overstepped their authority when criticized by those who supported segregation. The reverse position was equally true. By examining the ministers' statement, we see how particular fault lines develop concerning ministerial engagement and why those engagements can be both helpful and futile at the same moment. Though it is possible to make too much out of this skirmish between politics and religion, the fact that it has been largely ignored as little more than "going on record" suggests that we have yet to understand its significance. Numan Bartley noted that his "tentative" interpretations of southern institutions like churches should be followed by more study of those groups. Few, however, have taken up Bartley's challenge to examine these institutions more fully.[1] In Richmond, as well as other places across the South, a group of ministers entered the marketplace of ideas and altered the politics of segregation, even if they did not desegregate society as a whole.

The Region's Ministers Speak Out

Given that the Gainesville Ministerial Association had anticipated the struggle between preachers and politicians over desegregation before *Brown*, "statements" scattered across the southern landscape for more than three years should not surprise us. While the tone and content of the statements were similar, the context shaped the attention the promulgation each received. The Gainesville ministers barely made a blip on the radar. This pattern repeated itself in places where ministers supported the local school board's decision to open schools on a desegregated basis in 1956 (such as Warrenton, Virginia). Ministers in Macon, Georgia, gathered to "examine" the desegregation question, but little more was said about their raising the issue or whether their examination led to any solutions.[2] In the immediate aftermath of *Brown*, the muted responses may have led to nondescript concerns regarding ministerial pronouncements since it was unclear how southern states would respond. By the time massive resistance forces found a direction and headed full speed to circumvent the US Supreme Court's order of "all deliberate speed," however, ministerial pronouncements became roadblocks for segregationists, and for the ministerial organizations.

Almost nine months after the Richmond ministers entered the political fray concerning desegregation, a white Protestant ministerial association in Atlanta took up the issue and released two statements, the first in late 1957 and the second in 1958. The second, a six-point plan, coincided with the Soviet Union's launch of Sputnik II and the space dog Curly.[3] Whether due to the launch, which commanded significant attention, or growing tensions in Little Rock, the statement prompted little reaction. On November 4, the Atlanta *Constitution* editorialized on the statement, emphasizing the ministers' measured approach. Reader comments equaled the number of reports and editorials, which were only a few. So little attention was paid to the statement that later historical references to the Atlanta ministers' opposition to segregation did not mention any Atlanta newspaper but credited the *New York Times*' November 3 report.[4]

The Atlanta ministers outlined a strategy that other ministerial associations would use in the efforts to undercut massive resistance. The white ministers demanded that the First Amendment be safeguarded as a way to deal with the restrictive measures southern states were placing on groups like the NAACP. The proclamation also asked that Georgia "obey" the nation's laws, but also change them using legal strategies. The ministers argued for keeping the public schools open in the face of desegregation. They also admonished Georgians to resist violence and hate, and they hoped that "leaders of the races" would maintain open communication. Finally, the ministers also asked that prayer guide all future action.[5] In this foray into the political arena, the Atlanta ministers asserted a moral claim to the desegregation crisis, but they did not directly challenge Georgia's governor or the state legislature. It appeared the ministers could claim a victory for desegregation but the moderated language meant that every social issue could be addressed the same way: obey the law, protect liberties, and pray for guidance. The lack of response to the ministers highlights a difference between the Richmond ministers "manifesto" and the Atlanta statements. In the context of Richmond, ministerial assertion into the public arena found both a stern rebuttal against desegregation from segregation advocates, but oddly they also found favor among white southerners ready to change the culture of the Jim Crow South.

Richmond Ministers Go On Record

Like the VCHR's campaign in the period just after *Brown*, the RMA asserted a moral claim on the actions of the special session of the General Assembly. Unlike the VCHR, whose membership had religious connections but carried no specific religious authority, the RMA's position on the actions of the governor and the legislature carried with it a certain power to shape public opinion. Although these architects of improved race relations failed to desegregate Richmond, they succeeded in defining a moral case against segregation in Richmond's religious consciousness. An examination of the confrontation between the RMA and the proponents of massive resistance elucidates the ways in which ministers tackled several important challenges to their position as moral guardians to a new racial order. The way the Richmond newspapers attacked the ministerial group, and the effects those attacks had on members, reveals the limited effect of the ministers' social engagement with segregation.

Some within the RMA had intended all along to be a presence on the sociopolitical scene regarding race relations, as Marion's speech in 1953 made clear. Meeting in October 1956, the RMA made plans to call attention to the work of Stanley and the General Assembly during the special session of August and September 1956. The executive committee of the RMA worked for three months to draft a "statement" intended to focus attention on the moral claim in the desegregation controversy. Members of the executive committee came from the association's officers and committee heads. The following ministers were members of the executive committee: Dr. Frederick H. Olert, Second Presbyterian (white); Dr. J. S. Johnston, Reveille Methodist (white); Rev. Edward J. Humphrey, Westminster Presbyterian (white); Dr. John M. Ellison, past president of Virginia Union University (black); Rev. Wayne Bell, Seventh Street Christian (white); Dr. C. Levering Evans, Virginia Union University (black); Rev. Owen Weatherly, Second Baptist (white); Rev. W. A. Rogers, Laburnum Presbyterian (white). Reports conflicted on who drafted the statement. If it was as the *Richmond Times-Dispatch* indicated on the day the statement was published, then black and white ministers worked together. The same newspaper one day later noted a comment by Dr. Joe Johnston, the newly elected president of the group, stating the group's white members drafted the statement.[6] At the ministers' January 1957 meeting with sixty members present, the executive committee offered a 1,500-word statement for consideration by the association. On the first vote, three "'noes' against" the resolution were heard. However, by the final vote only one voted against the pronouncement.[7] After agreeing to the content of the manifesto, the ministers bought advertising space in the *Richmond Times-Dispatch* to publish the Statement of Conviction. Although they did not individually sign the document and refused to name those present at the January 28 meeting, the very public nature of the ad placed the RMA at the center of the public debate over desegregation.

The "forthright appeal for racial equality" condemned the actions of the governor and the General Assembly during the 1956 special session.[8] Calling on the General Assembly to rescind the massive resistance laws, the statement invoked the authority of God over the temporal order. Any law that inhibited a person's inherent rights violated God's will. The ministers argued that Governor Stanley and the special session of the General Assembly had failed to understand the gravity of their actions. Democratic principles played as significant a role as biblical exposition concerning morally upright race relations. Quoting Washington, Jefferson, and Madison rather than Jesus and St. Paul, the ministers claimed that God's purposes in American life naturally led to the fulfillment of the democratic promises of the American founders. The opening lines of the document wedded these two ideas together. "This," it claimed, "is God's world. It operates under God's laws. Men either learn these laws, live in obedience to them and prosper, or they ignore their stern reality, follow selfish devices and suffer. Men may not change these laws." The ministers closed the preamble of their statement with a harsh rebuke to those who walked outside of God's laws. "We must," they admonished, "live in God's world, in God's way, or we perish."[9]

After declaring God's dominion over the works of creation, the ministers reminded Richmonders of Virginia's place within the democratic ideal. Again intertwining religion and politics in Virginia, the statement boasted, "political philosophy and religious conviction have seldom been divorced." Elucidating this concept, the writers outlined their Christian notion of political expression. Virginia's "greatness has stemmed from its repeated enunciation of such basic ideas as the reality of man's dependence upon Divine Providence; the inherent worth and dignity of the individual citizen as a child of God; and the consequent rights of men as individuals in society." Recognizing Virginia's own failure at the democratic ideal, the statement added that "at its best" the tradition in Virginia had upheld "individual freedom, equality of opportunity, justice before the law, and many other ideals precious to mankind" in opposition to "tyranny of body and soul." Calling on the great pantheon of Virginia leaders—Washington, Jefferson, Madison, Marshall, and Monroe—the ministers' statement connected the democratic ideal to God's providence and defended religious engagement with the political process. "Each [of these men]," the statement asserted, "in his own way brought to national leadership the convictions of gentlemen bred in the milieu of democratic culture. Each insisted that the religious faith of that culture from which he had come find embodiment in the important legislative act of the nation."[10]

While the writers of the statement performed some historical hyperbole, the RMA's document called legislators to faithful commitment, to revival so to speak, by appealing to the religious undertone of American democratic belief. They asserted what Myrdal referred to as the American Creed. Democratic principles could no longer be confined to church polity but extended to the sovereign rights of every individual, including the country's black citizens. The more subtle argument the ministers made involved God's working through the democratic ideal. Without saying it outright, the ministers implied that race and slavery had played a major role in diminishing the ideal. Yet, the very nature of "we hold these truths to be self-evident, that all men are created equal" came not just from Jefferson but also through God's prompting of the great thinker. Here the ministers tied the political actions of the past to divine command. Jefferson's limited vision in the eighteenth century could be fulfilled in the twentieth century, if only citizens could see God's plan. Any impediment of that plan could bring God's judgment. For this reason, the ministers argued, what God granted only God could take away. The ministers' statement made clear that their protest against the unjust legislative acts was appropriate in a democratic society, particularly one that supposedly valued religion.

The reason for this rhetorical step becomes apparent in the third section of their document. Recalling the events of the previous fall, the statement added that the bills passed by the General Assembly amounted to being undemocratic and un-Christian. The target of their attack included House Bill No. 60. Also known as the "anti-NAACP" bill, which by 1957 was law, the legislation required "race" groups such as the NAACP and the Ku Klux Klan to register with a newly formed state commission, to release their mailing lists, and to refrain from any civil suits designed to circumvent the legislative acts of the General Assembly (e.g., suing school districts on behalf of black children to gain access to white schools as in *Brown*) or any attempt to influence legislative action on behalf of the race question.[11] Proponents had claimed that it required the same information from the Defenders of State Sovereignty and Individual Liberties, Virginia's version of a white citizen's council. The defenders organization quickly complied with the new law by sending its mailing lists to the state oversight committee. In bold terms, the ministers' indicted both the governor and the General Assembly for their actions concerning desegregation, and specifically House Bill No. 60. They asserted "the point of our concern is that the present governor and a majority of the Legislature have, in our opinion, seriously impaired the sacred and historic traditions of Virginia democracy and lowered the prestige of the state in the eyes of thoughtful people all across the nation, if not the world, by what we regard as their exceedingly inept handling of the current racial situation."[12] The ministers understood the intent of the massive resistance laws was to intimidate and harass black citizens, who wanted their right to quality education. Since the intent of the laws was to do harm, the RMA cried out against the injustice.

The pronouncement, however, was not simply a rhetorical attack against the governor and legislative leaders. The ministers advocated specific steps that would remedy the situation. First, the anti-NAACP laws needed to be rescinded. Second, Virginia had to comply with the US Supreme Court's decisions and further efforts to avoid desegregation had to stop. Third, the ministers argued that "community rights are as vital as states rights" and therefore local option should be implemented. Fourth, a school system equitable to all Virginia citizens had to be constructed with "all deliberate speed" to replace the current segregated system. Fifth, and perhaps the boldest part of the statement, the removal of all social customs violating the dignity of the Negro had to be eradicated. In a note that showed the ministers' unwillingness to concede the rhetorical war over desegregation, they added, "The passing away of these irritating customs does not involve inter-marriage or amalgamation of the races; it declares a wholesome respect for all people and evidences common courtesy." The statement closed in a defiant tone. "At the proper time and in the right place," it said, "we commit ourselves to make the weight of our convictions felt and to help restore our state to the stature among states from which, in our opinion, she has recently fallen."[13]

In reporting on the statement, the *Richmond News Leader* appeared to undermine the clergy's credibility by reporting that not all Richmond ministers supported the RMA's position. The paper quoted the Rev. Rufus J. Womble, a priest at the Church of the Epiphany, saying, "coerced integration was equally as bad as coerced segregation." Echoing a refrain among many concerning religious intrusion into the political realm, he said: "The hearts and minds of people must change before we can get far with integration."[14] The fact that the news report got one minister to go on record against the RMA's statement suggested, the report hinted, that there was a division within ministerial ranks. The staff writer, however, placed very little context around the quotation, so the reader has to infer whether Womble stands against desegregation or simply did not think this particular tact would move desegregation forward. One might have thought that Rev. Womble cast the dissenting vote at the RMA meeting, which he did not. The quotation, however, allowed the *Richmond News Leader* to paint a picture of a divided clergy, with the unnamed sixty representing a minority of Richmond area clergy.

Richmond's Newspapers Respond

The *Richmond Times-Dispatch* led with a front-page story on the same day of the published "statement." Readers came across the news article before reading the statement itself, which appeared on page two. The RMA's "Conviction on Race" evoked the ire of both of Richmond's white newspaper editors. Kilpatrick led the charge. In the January 30 *Richmond News Leader*, he devoted nearly three-quarters of the editorial space to the statement. Kilpatrick claimed the ministers were right to single out the anti-NAACP laws and called for rescinding it. However, he lambasted the clergy for the cloak of secrecy around the meeting. If they really stood by their conviction, they would have signed the statement. "If editors, publishers and lawmakers" Kilpatrick wrote, "are expected to express their opinions openly and over their own signatures, no good reason suggests itself why the individual clergymen who approved this statement should not have done so over their names."

His most biting commentary about the statement involved the ministers' lack of historical perspective. Kilpatrick pointed out that the great political heritage they spoke of came at the price of human bondage. He also attacked the notion that desegregation was a moral issue. Since the court's order dealt with temporal laws, he concluded, "the ministers are again confusing that which is mortal with that which is divine." The last harangue he saved for the idea that the court held final authority for interpreting the supreme law of the land. "In the case immediately at bar," Kilpatrick wrote, "the people-as-States long ago agreed that the Fourteenth Amendment was not intended to prohibit the States from operating racially separate schools."[15] The hypocrisy in his diatribe against the clergy's misappropriation of history was that he fell victim to a static view of constitutional interpretation. The US Supreme Court ruled in 1896 that only segregated railcars were legal; southern states following the lead of federal circuit court rulings *interpreted* the separate but equal benchmark to apply to all institutions where racial interaction might occur, including schools. By 1954, the court had undergone an interpretative transformation that rendered its earlier decision null and void with regard to education, a point Kilpatrick refused to acknowledge.[16] As one commentator pointed out, he played loose with the facts and "edit[ed] some one hundred years of constitutional growth out of American history."[17] Kilpatrick attempted to deny the ministers' argument on the basis of faulty logic. In trying to neutralize the effect, he must have sensed what segregationists began to assert in the late 1950s: vast numbers of ministers would not support the segregationist cause.[18]

The editorial position of the *Richmond Times-Dispatch* reiterated Kilpatrick's tone in its own editorial on the morning of January 31. Agreeing that the anti-NAACP laws violated certain rights, the *Richmond Times-Dispatch* called the legislation and its intended effect an "extremely dubious and dangerous procedure." Yet it also criticized the fifty-nine ministers who voted for the statement. The newspaper called attention to the ministers' claim that where a law did not "violate a moral or religious principle" it must be adhered to. The editorial retorted, "who is to decide when there is a violation of a moral or religious principle? Is this to be determined by less than 10 per cent of Richmond's Protestant clergy, irrespective of the views of the other 90 per cent, or of the laymen who constitute the congregations of the clergymen concerned?" The newspaper opined that it hoped the clergy understood the complexity of the issue and that "men of good will are to be found on both sides of this sundering question."[19] The RMA's moral indignation carried little weight with the two city newspapers. As the ministers made their moral claim, the first line of attack by segregationists involved belittling them. It was the "complexity" of the issue that forced the ministers who agreed to the document and voted for its release to raise the importance of the moral claim. As the campaign against the ministers' statement dragged out, Richmonders soon found out that far more than ten percent of the ministerial ranks supported the cause.

In the week following the release of the statement, the two papers published no fewer than twenty-nine "letters to the editor" from readers. Two Richmond ministers had their dissenting opinions aired. George J. Cleaveland, pastor of the Church of the Ascension, Episcopal, wrote that he wanted to "disassociate" himself from the statement. Noting that he was not present at the January 28 meeting, he stated: "I do not accept certain of the theological statements therein, I do not associate myself with the interpretation therein of the motives and actions of the Governor and legislators, and I do not consider myself sufficiently acquainted with the content and purport of the legislation enacted by the Virginia Assembly at its recent sessions to speak with finality about it."

Cleaveland also informed the Richmond readers that his position should not be understood as an endorsement of "any position which advocates any form of injustice towards Negroes."[20] This strange mediated public position has led interpreters of the period to assume a closed position on desegregation when in disagreement with prophetic positions.

Another Episcopal priest, G. MacLaren Brydon (retired), went a step further in condemning the statement. Unlike Cleaveland, Brydon wanted people to know that the ministers had crossed a sacred line. "The most serious fact about this statement," he wrote, "is that the ministers as a group are seeking to influence and direct action of the state Legislature in a matter of civil government." In a move designed to show how misguided clergy can violate the strict wall of separation between church and state, Brydon harkened back to Virginia's history with "political" ministers. "With the remembrance among students of Virginia's history of Parson Massey in the Readjuster era [1880s] and of Bishop Cannon in our more recent past," he argued, "I do not think that our people of today are willing to give to the clergy of the state any more influence in political life than the individual influence of each man as an individual citizen."[21] Brydon rejected the historical account of the ministers' statement and claimed that Virginia held the most positive of relations between the races. "Certainly I speak for Virginia," he claimed in a grandiose tone, "when I say that there are and have been for the past two generations hundreds of thousands of white people in our state who are genuinely interested in the welfare of the Negro race. . . . And there has grown up an understanding friendship between white and Negro which has helped the Negro race to develop as much as it has, and which is the hope of years to come."[22] This paternalistic approach to race relations has also commanded the attention of historians.

Ministerial objections underwhelmed those of the laity. Divided equally among men and women, the comments that made it to print generally involved condemnation of preachers meddling into political business and asserted accusations that the preachers wanted "amalgamation" of the races. One letter writer made a direct connection between the statement and the legal challenge to segregation by the National Association for the Advancement of Colored People. "Next to the NAACP," she wrote, "ministers have done more to create tension between the races than any other group of citizens." A second letter writer heaped the entire ministerial association together with other perceived "liberal" people. In sarcastic fashion, he wrote: "A short, simple statement by them that they have now adopted Earl Warren as the guiding light and from now and here on preach the doctrine of Herbert Lehman, Eleanor Roosevelt, the ADA and the NAACP would have covered the subject in full." Acknowledging the lack of desegregation in Richmond churches and perhaps catching the ministerial association at its most vulnerable spot, yet another letter writer inquired whether desegregation would be more appropriately fostered in churches than public schools. "This brotherhood stuff," he wrote, "belongs, peculiarly, to the church. Would it not be more consistent if the present head of the Ministers' Association, the Rev. Mr. Johnston, set the pace and established at his church mixed Sunday school classes?"[23]

One, however, objected to the criticism the ministers would receive. Calling the statement "intelligent and Christian," the writer voiced concern that the ministers would not be taken seriously and that their effort might be discounted. Using the language of the critics, the letter noted, "Some will yell, 'Preachers ought to stick to religion.'" Yet, the writer believed the ministers were correct to make their stand *because of* their religion. "Such critics—and there will be many—fail to see that religion, instead of being an isolated area of one's personality, is the motivating force in life. It determines the values by which a man lives, and of the varied aspects of existence. A man's religion manifests itself in all of one's attitudes toward and relations with his fellow man—or else his religion is nothing."[24] The letter writer agreed with the actions of the group of ministers who affirmed the statement because, like John Marion, he saw a direct correlation between faith claims and God's providence here on earth. For the letter writer, religious teaching informed political activity; it served as a form of witness.

Because the anonymity of the statement's authorship had garnered so much attention, the *Richmond Times-Dispatch* decided to run a survey of Richmond area ministers to find out who supported the statement. The *Richmond Times-Dispatch* wanted to put the ministers on the spot. Though the survey might have been newsworthy on its own, the editorial stance of the paper and the political climate of the time suggested otherwise. The informal telephone survey reached three-hundred-and-eighty-two ministers in Central Virginia.[25] It is unclear whether the ministers knew that their name and church affiliation would be published in the paper, although the large number of "no comments" suggests some did. The survey, dominated by Baptists, contacted all sectors of Richmond and the surrounding counties' ministerial community except Catholic priests because as the paper suggested "the Catholic Church has already announced its stand on racial integration."[26] The *Richmond Times-Dispatch* noted that it contacted one-hundred-and-eighty members of the RMA, non-RMA members made up the remainder of the survey. The news article stated that over three-hundred-and-seventy were contacted, but it was unclear why the report shorted the count by twelve, which their own numbers bear out. Two-hundred-and-two RMA and non-RMA members agreed either with the statement wholly or with qualification, which made up just under fifty-three percent of those contacted. Forty-eight RMA and non-RMA members rejected either wholly or with qualification the RMA's stand, which made up over twelve percent of those contacted. One-hundred-and-thirty-two ministers answered "no comment" when asked, which represented thirty-four percent. It appeared that the newspaper saw the survey as a way to pin ministers on the controversial subject and perhaps point out how few ministers really supported the Statement of Conviction.[27]

Numan Bartley asserted that "any minister, no matter how small his plant, could recognize the fact that silence was golden, or at least that there was some relationship between silence and gold."[28] Some ministers may have in fact deferred to "no comment" to escape the wrath of a congregation. The tactics of the newspaper "survey," however, provide a possible explanation for the large number of "no comments." The *Richmond Times-Dispatch* made calls from listings in the Richmond directory. Without always clearly identifying what the purpose of the phone call was, some ministers refrained from a commitment. In the case of Rev. Irving Elligan, the first black Presbyterian minister in Richmond and pastor of All Souls Presbyterian Church in Barton Heights, he did not fear the repercussions of an angry congregation but realistically could be cautious with his name and opinion in a public forum of a hostile environment, including a number of ministers in the presbytery who did not condone the statement. John Ensign, director of Camps and Conferences for Hanover Presbytery, indicated "no comment" at the very moment he was preparing to open the presbytery's summer camps on a desegregated basis the following summer. The paper announced that at the same meeting that approved the statement that Dr. Joseph Johnston was also voted the RMA's new president. He defended the statement in the news article but answered the survey "no comment." Like Ensign, Johnston would play a key role in advocating for desegregated churches in the years ahead, challenging his bishop in the process. There were, therefore, a number of ministers on the "no comment" list who held desegregation sympathies given their other affiliations, so more than fifty-five percent of area ministers were sympathetic to desegregation and worked to advocate for it. The survey backfired and Dabney, Kilpatrick, and segregationists had their answer: a majority of Richmond's clergy supported the *Brown* decision.

Implications for Ministerial Engagement

The writers of the RMA statement and those who voted to support it saw moral implications in the massive resistance laws. Speaking against those injustices appeared imperative. Yet the statement, like the call by the religious editors to vote against the referendum, had little binding effect upon churchgoers and even less on those who did not attend church. The freedom of individual conscience dictated political action more than church teaching. James J. Kilpatrick served as a case in point. As a Catholic, he espoused an open contempt for desegregation of schools in the pages of the *Richmond News Leader* and racist tendencies in his personal correspondence.[29] The Richmond editor's opinion stood in direct contradiction with his bishop, which the *Richmond Times-Dispatch* pointed out when it said the Catholic bishop had already stated the Catholic position in favor of desegregation. Kilpatrick did finally leave the Catholic Church, but not without first standing in opposition to its ecclesiastical authority. If he could exert such a strong, and public, conviction based on individual conscience within the perceived control of the diocesan hierarchy, how much more freedom existed in less centralized denominations.

This interpretation of the statement resembles the pattern that Ernest Campbell and Thomas Pettigrew found in Little Rock, Arkansas, when they studied ministerial responses to the desegregation crisis of 1957 and 1958 in that city. In their study, Campbell and Pettigrew quoted a minister as saying that the "staggering fact [is] that the Church is largely without influence in the day of society's trouble." While individualism was an important component in attempting to get a congregation to heed a prophetic voice on race, the bigger problem for ministers-as-social-reformers was the influence of conscience on changing social patterns.[30] By locating authority in individual conscience, ministers and denominational entities could only go so far in causing change because individuals, who make up the congregation or denominational body, could object based on their conscience without jeopardizing their place in the religious community. If people felt their consciences had been violated, they simply withdrew their memberships in the voluntary association.[31] An important aspect of this shift, however, meant that persuasion became the only tool for religious leaders.

Critics of the RMA's Statement of Conviction thought the ministers had overstepped their bounds and "meddled" in politics where preachers did not belong. Historians, however sympathetic they may be, have argued that the statement meant little more than "going on record" against segregation.[32] In terms of overt political resistance, the RMA statement failed. Only after large numbers of white Virginia citizens became disillusioned with the draconian tactics of massive resistance did some semblance of sanity return to Virginia politics.[33]

The Statement of Conviction, however, put segregationist politicians on notice: ministers would not create a theological justification for segregation. The RMA's statement was not intended to dictate social policy. The use of the document as a means for social reform would be inappropriate. Rather than take on a legislative body, which they tried to do in 1953, the ministers issued a public statement. It was clear by the plan they laid out that they expected some political change. More important, however, the statement created an alternative vision of southern morality—or at the very least, Virginia race relations. Though the ministers may have hoped that the state legislators would change their minds, they asserted that a number of ministers in Richmond would not provide a theological foundation for the further oppression of African Americans.[34] Without this support, the massive resistance campaign was doomed to failure. David Chappell in his insightful look at the "divided mind" of segregationists has argued that "the crucial ingredient that was missing from the segregationist movement was a rich, confident, biblical argument promulgated by their clergymen."[35] While those voices were present in places in the South, their marginal status limited their power, as Pettigrew and Campbell pointed out in Little Rock. Richmond's ministers were ready to proclaim a gospel that supported desegregated public schools.

While we may debate the effect that ministerial or denominational pronouncements have on the general public, the pronouncements intended to instruct the faithful and create an alternative understanding of God's purposes in this world. The RMA, through its statement, declared that its members would not serve as activists or ideologues for segregationists in their struggle against desegregation. As one segregationist in Virginia put it, "The worst obstacle we face in the fight to preserve segregated schools in the South is the white preacher." He added: "The patriots of Reconstruction had the preachers praying for them instead of working against them."[36] Historians miss the subtle importance of this ministerial pronouncement by focusing on the political outcome. Rather than see it as a failed attempt at social influence, which most of the objectors at the time thought, this manifesto allowed the ministers to enter the public debate and assert a moral claim distinct from the understood cultural norm. In bold terms, the ministers made clear that the forces of massive resistance failed to see the moral dimensions of their actions. A majority of Richmond ministers asserted that the churches would not give theological credence to oppression. Unlike a century earlier when ministers defended the cause of slavery as a God-ordained system, these ministers would make no such claim about segregation. They may not have dictated public policy, but they did serve as voices for a different vision on race relations. The statement acted as a witness to cultural transformation, but the ministers understood that ultimately the change came through personal revelation. The outward sign of this revelation found a political expression in what ministers like John Marion referred to as a "magnificent obsession."

The RMA's Statement of Conviction revealed three important factors in Richmond's religious attitude toward desegregation. First, the manifesto articulated a strong sense of purpose—prophetic in nature—among area ministers to distance themselves from the restrictive actions of ardent segregationists. Second, for a city as infused with symbolic memory as Richmond, the ministers went "on record" to denounce the continued oppression of black citizens in Virginia, particularly in schools, and in prohibiting their free assembly. Third, while the ministers may have been ready to withdraw their support of cultural inequalities, the people in the pews and a few of their colleagues saw little need to equate the struggles of school desegregation with the life of their churches.

Barton Heights Baptist Church, which by 1957 was Northminster Baptist Church, and Overbrook Presbyterian Church showed how individual congregations, acting as moral communities, dealt with the consequences of residential desegregation, which in turn created the potential for school desegregation in cities, by moving out. Northminster went a few miles north of its 1950 location, but Overbrook moved more than thirty minutes northwest into Henrico County. The ministerial pronouncement established a viable moral alternative to segregation, but left the messy details of what that meant to individual congregations and denominations. The "survey" taken by the *Richmond Times-Dispatch* and the "letters to the editor" of both white Richmond newspapers also exposed the variety of responses by ministers and the laity to the statement. Minsters and segregationists alike knew that as long as churches and denominations remained segregated, the prophetic call of the church to social equality appeared hypocritical. Richmond area Presbyterians and Methodists spent the remainder of the 1950s trying to come to grips with this contradiction by putting their houses in order. The ensuing struggles exposed the extent to which white congregations were limited in the way they could lead in changing attitudes regarding desegregation.

5
THE LIMITS OF CHANGE

In the November elections of 1957 and 1958, Virginia voters appeared to endorse the massive resistance campaign of the Byrd organization.[1] Senator Byrd's reelection to the Senate by an overwhelming majority should have confirmed to the citizens of Virginia and the nation that no public school in Virginia would be desegregated any time soon. Through legislative actions in 1956 and 1957, Virginia's governor had gained, and exercised, broad powers to circumvent any locality from desegregating its schools. Virginia's massive resisters removed any possibility that the unsightly events in Little Rock would occur in the Old Dominion. Any black child seeking admission to a white school had to go through a placement board; if the placement board agreed to the child's admission, the governor could override the board's decision by ordering the school to be closed.[2]

Interestingly, it took until July 1958 for a black student to seek admission to a white school in Richmond.[3] Oliver Hill, the NAACP lawyer involved in the Prince Edward desegregation case, wrote a letter on July 3 to the city school board informing the board that three black children asked him to petition on their behalf to attend the white elementary school near their home in Richmond's East-end during the upcoming school year. In an article in the *Richmond News Leader*, Hill said the families of the children requested that he use "whatever legal steps necessary to secure their admission." Kilpatrick responded with an emotionally charged editorial to the petition. "There can be but one answer," he demanded, "and that answer is no." Having wished that black people could have been more patient for upgraded schools, Kilpatrick informed his readers that the day of tribulation, something he predicted in 1951, had come for Richmond. "The hope [for segregated public schools in Richmond]," he lamented, "was vain." The editor warned of the dire consequences to follow and then added his harshest criticism to date. "Richmond," Kilpatrick fumed, "is in for trouble now, and we may as well face the fact calmly and resolutely, determined to abandon every public school in Richmond, white and black alike, before we surrender even one room to integration."[4]

Richmond religious leaders did not remain silent during the state school closings of 1958, though their voices often found expression through nonreligious organizations like the Committee for Public Schools (CPS). The Richmond area CPS president was Dr. James Syndor, a professor at the Presbyterian School for Christian Education. The advisory board had several prominent religious leaders among its ranks. Mrs. Theodore Adams, wife of Theodore Adams (First Baptist's pastor), joined the crusade as she had in other endeavors like the Virginia Council on Human Relations. Adele Clark, who also served on the board, believed in the cause of desegregated public schools from her Catholic position on divine imperative and natural law. Several clergy also participated. Rev. C. Levering Evans, pastor at Weatherford Memorial Baptist, which opened its membership on an integrated basis in 1960, and Dr. Joseph S. Johnston, pastor at Reveille Methodist, who headed the Richmond Ministers' Association during the publication of its Statement of Conviction, both made courageous stands in favor of desegregation.[5]

As the struggle over desegregating public schools took on national significance in light of Little Rock, Richmond churches began to struggle with their own culpability in the desegregation controversy. Segregationists were prone to point out the hypocrisy of white church leaders calling for desegregation of schools—as the RMA's statement had done—when their own flocks remained lily-white. By the mid-1950s, most southern mainline denominations were "on record" supporting the desegregation of public schools and church organizations. Little visible change in segregated congregations, however, had occurred. To understand this phenomenon we will examine two Protestant bodies in Richmond—Presbyterians and Methodists—and their encounter with desegregation. The internal debates within each group show how white Christians in Richmond grappled with the gospel message of brotherhood and their cultural identity of separatism. Rather than retreating, these engagements uncover churches' efforts to struggle critically against the surrounding segregated culture, even as some continued to embrace a vision of separated kingdoms.

Presbyterians and Methodists

From 1957 to 1959, white Richmonders grappled with what it meant for the clergy to express a prophetic voice for desegregation of public schools even as their own congregations and denominations remained segregated. The internal strife marked both a beginning and an end. For the first time since the early 1800s, white denominations had to deal with the question of the equal status of black members in the church. As noted, Richmond Catholics had the parish system, which included ethnic parishes for African Americans, to insulate them from conversations over desegregating their congregations. They would, however, show the limits of integration as the hierarchy chose to close black parishes and fold them into white parishes. The agitation for equal access for African Americans never meant losing cultural identity, though that was almost always what happened when white citizens controlled the desegregation process. Virginia Baptists had made the choice in the aftermath of the American Civil War to worship and to serve separately. Even when black Baptists attempted some form of reconciliation in the 1870s, white Baptists set their sights on separate denominational structures with almost no crossing of the color line. Individuals and congregations did reach across the divide, but in episodic ways. In Richmond, the discussion about desegregating public schools, however, began to shift discussions to appropriate responses by denominational agencies and leaders concerning desegregation in church life. Both Virginia Methodists and Richmond Presbyterians had black adherents within their respective denominational structures but had not fully integrated them into organizational life. As both bodies struggled to understand the prophetic call impelling them to a broader understanding of desegregation, priestly forces pushed back to defend their beloved institutions. In the midst of the debates, there were some priests who became prophets.

The fighting revealed the complex nature of the church as an agent of social change. The tensions shook these communities of faith long before direct action of young black leaders conspired to challenge their commitment to the gospel of reconciliation. The internal debates would give way to the direct action protests of the civil rights movement in the 1960s, but the battle lines within white churches had already been drawn.

Virginia Methodists: Limits of Priestly Impulses

Virginia Methodist pastors and their bishop fought over the general subject of desegregation. At the governor's side in 1955, Bishop Paul N. Garber of the Virginia Conference showed an affinity with segregationists but remained publicly ambivalent about the possibility of the church leading the way on civil rights. George Reamey, editor of the *Virginia Methodist Advocate*, served up what at first appeared to be bland editorial pronouncements: Christians should love their neighbors but the court overstepped its authority in the *Brown* decision. Bishop Garber and Reamey, however, shared similarly held strong opinions against desegregation and that brought them into conflict with Richmond-area Methodist ministers.

Shortly after the *Brown* decision, George Reamey began a crusade in the pages of the *Virginia Methodist Advocate* to help Virginia Methodists understand that the US Supreme Court had failed to understand the gravity of its change in position regarding "separate but equal." Reamey's priestly impulse to maintain cultural norms allowed him to embrace a segregated society but challenge perceived church–state threats. And although the *Virginia Methodist Advocate* was the official organ of the conference, it appeared that Bishop Garber allowed for some amount of freedom within his jurisdiction on matters of conscience. What remained unclear in the early part of the public debate over desegregation was whether Reamey, through the *Virginia Methodist Advocate*, spoke for the bishop or maintained editorial distance and aired his own views. The evidence from personal correspondence from both Reamey and Garber makes clear that by 1956 what the *Virginia Methodist Advocate* published as its editorial position was privately held by Garber.

In the fall of 1956, Bishop Garber participated in a public panel discussion about desegregation from a Christian perspective. As part of its multipart series on the question of desegregation in the South *Life* magazine published a transcript of Garber's round-table discussion with other representatives from southern Protestant denominations. Under the banner headline, "A Round Table Has Debate on Christians' Moral Duty," *Life* allowed southern Christians the opportunity to speak to the nation on their own behalf about Christian responsibility toward desegregation.[6] The magazine ran the round-table discussion alongside an article written by evangelist Billy Graham that openly condemned segregation as un-Christian.[7] Stanley High, senior editor at *Reader's Digest*, moderated the discussion. Two individuals represented Southern Baptists: Duke McCall, president of Southern Baptist Theological Seminary, and A. C. Miller, executive secretary of the Commission on Christian Relations of the Southern Baptist Convention. Mrs. Spann W. Milner, vice president of United Church Women, was the only woman present. L. Nelson Bell, former member of Presbyterian World Mission Board, acted as the Presbyterian voice. Bishop Henry Irving Louttit, Episcopal bishop of South Florida, spoke on behalf of Episcopalians from southern Florida. And along with Garber, Methodists also had Edwin Jones, executive committee member of the World Methodist Council.[8] Individuals have limited ability to speak on behalf of entire groups, particularly when personal theology and denominational policy rub against one another. Though the point of the gathering was to take the pulse of religious bodies in the South, much of what occurred in the case of Garber involved his personal sentiment regarding segregation. The meeting also showed how unlikely it would be that white Christians in the South would reach a consensus regarding desegregation.

As moderator, Stanley High led the group through three phases of discussion. First, he inquired about the authority of scripture over segregation. Edwin Jones of the World Methodist Council started the conversation by stating that God had in fact wanted separate races and for them to stay separated: why else would God require the Jewish people to remain a separate people? Bishop Louttit pointed out that the biblical command to remain separate had to do with national issues and not simply racial issues. Nelson Bell introduced the quandary presented by using biblical texts to support a particular position, indicating that many desegregationists might point to Acts 17:26, where the apostle Paul entreats the Greeks to recognize that God has made all of humankind from "one blood." He, however, also pointed out that segregationists go to the next verse to show that God intended the races to be separated, citing Paul's cryptic phrase: "the bounds of their habitation." The different uses of Paul's single sermon at Mars Hill to both defend and attack desegregation showed that biblical authority rested with the interpreter's predisposition rather than any moral authority asserted by the text on its own. Mrs. Milner, Dr. Miller, Dr. McCall, and Bishop Louttit all spoke in defense of a more open posture in race relations between black and white people, including the churches. Stanley High took this majority opinion to address the next issue: the place of church activity on race relations *prior* to the *Brown* decision.[9]

Though Bishop Garber did not speak to the first issue raised by the round-table participants, he quickly stated his position with regard to the *Brown* decision. Speaking first, Garber resorted to a rhetorical device often used by southerners uncomfortable with desegregation, stating: "a black person said . . . ." Noting that less than a week after the court's decision, the president of a leading "Negro educational institution" claimed that without the leadership of the churches, the US Supreme Court decision would not have been possible. Garber went on to read, at length, the statement made by the Methodist General Conference concerning Methodists and proper race relations, which included the need for Methodists to stand at the forefront of desegregation. He, however, pointed out the limitation of the conference's action when he added, "It should be understood that this resolution of the General Conference does not bind congregations or individuals." Garber claimed, "The final decision within Methodism on this and other similar problems rests with each individual member."[10] What appeared to bother Garber more than anything about the court's decision was the issue of forcing desegregation on an unwilling white South.

After a lengthy discussion about the role of churches in desegregation and southern life, which divided participants along lines similar to the matter about biblical authority, Stanley High again indicated that the majority opinion—an active Christian faith leading southerners toward desegregation—was the clearest vision presented by the round-table participants on race relations in the South. Going so far as to say that every church should open its doors to everyone, High appeared to have missed, or flatly ignored, Garber's contention that even with the progressive stance taken by the Methodist General Conference, no Methodist church in the General Conference could be forced to integrate.

When High asked what role churches should play in the desegregation of schools, Garber offered, "I think that there is a point here which one must consider as a Christian as well as a citizen. And that is the question of force. This forced integration is a red flag to a great many people in the Southland. And it raises the question: is it really Christian to make white people integrate if they do not want to integrate?" He feared that desegregationists had not thought far enough ahead to foresee that complete desegregation would weaken the public school system. When one of the panelists indicated that black people might think that forced segregation had ruined the public school system, Garber contended that did not matter because in the end white people would abandon the public schools rather than face desegregation—a note not all that different from that of James Kilpatrick. Dr. McCall, president of Southern Baptist Theological Seminary, indicated that he agreed with Garber about the church involving itself too much in the world if segregation had not led to injustice, but when injustice occurred, as McCall believed it had, the church was morally obligated to act. Garber concurred on the importance of justice, but showed by his answer that he rejected that segregation reached an unbearable level of injustice. "I do not think," he argued, "that the church has to take a stand on every particular social and economic issue that comes up, or soon the church dissipates its strength for the great issues."[11] Sadly, Garber did not elaborate on what the "great issues" might be, as if desegregation was not one of them. He would later add during the discussion what appeared to be a contradiction to his position on the church's noninvolvement in school desegregation. "I think," Garber said, "the church is the spiritual basis for all social changes."[12] Again, he failed to enumerate what specific social changes the church could address from its spiritual position.

How could the church be an agent for social change from Garber's perspective? Since the "great issues" were left to the reader's imagination, one could claim that he had contradicted himself and therefore saw no earthly role in the life of the church. That contention, however, misses the point that conservative social change is still social change. Garber perceived, accurately, that an outside force would make both him and his flock bend to a social construction not of their liking. Since this outside force held no moral authority over him—a point he made clearly in the discussion—then his moral duty might be to stand against the alien authority, in this case the US Supreme Court.[13] As the initial question posed by the moderator at the round-table showed, no clear consensus existed among faithful believers in the South about what the authoritative text, the Bible, said concerning segregation. This lack of decisive meaning in the Bible concerning segregation and the authority of the individual believer's interpretation created the ambiguous response by some Christians to the plight of black school children. If the Bible meant anything to Bishop Garber, it meant that God had established the order and any change to that order constituted a breach that required resistance. Garber's "social change" occurred within the individual and could not be "forced" either on another individual or a community. At least in all things social, God had set the order in motion and engaged the individual, but rarely did God engage the society.[14] Garber's approach differed from those of Aubrey Brown and John Marion as well as other Methodist bishops, who believed God could speak through events of history and the lives of believers.

Virginia Methodist ministers tried to get their bishop to commit to desegregation without much success. Rev. Bruce Pate of Bridgeton, North Carolina, wrote to Garber in late January 1956 to ask for the bishop's comments on a sermon Pate had prepared concerning the church taking a leading role in better race relations. "I do not feel," Garber wrote back, "that I should make any comment on the sermon which you have sent to me. The freedom of the pulpit has been a cherished tradition in our Methodism. 'The Methodists think and let think' was stated long ago by John Wesley. Holding those sacred principles I would never in any way pass judgment upon the messages of our pastors."[15] Garber failed to mention to Pate that he regretted any association between the church and desegregation. In a telling response to a letter from a layman in North Carolina, Bishop Garber pleaded for understanding that he was fighting the righteous cause of segregation. Garber wrote, "I would appreciate it if you would permit me to talk to you about this entire matter. You would find that you and I hold almost identical views in regard to the NAACP and you would also come to understand that I have been leading the fight for our Southern viewpoint in the Council of Bishops. It is a little discouraging to have good laymen fail to support their bishop in his fight for our way of life. I have publicly stated that as long as I am bishop there is not going to be integration in the Methodist churches in Virginia."[16] Writing years later, his biographer considered Garber's public position on integration ambiguous at best.[17] The bishop's personal sentiment on segregation was clear.

Garber's guarded public stance on desegregation within the Virginia Conference became contentious in the summer of 1958. Early in July, George Reamey published an editorial in the *Virginia Methodist Advocate* titled "Integration and Moral Standards." Here, he asserted that all the talk concerning the US Supreme

Court's attempt to desegregate failed to address the most pressing problem: the differences in moral standards between black people and white people. To support his claim, Reamey introduced the Virginia State Bureau of Vital Statistics report on illegitimate births according to race from the previous year (1957). "The record," he wrote, "is one which we wish some of the ardent advocates of integration who speak for the general [Methodist] church would take time to read and digest. Our general church publications are filled with pleas for immediate integration on all levels on the specious ground that this is the only 'Christian' thing to do." Asking rhetorically, but pointedly, Reamey added, "Well, is it?" His answer was a resounding no.[18]

Quoting the number provided by the Bureau of Statistics, Reamey detailed the high percentage of illegitimate births among black Virginians—23.1 percent in 1957. After reporting a number—90,000 illegitimate black births from 1935 to 1957—he tried to distance his argument from the racist tone of other segregationists. "We are not prepared to say," Reamey added, "as some persons affirm, that this widespread difference in moral standards reflects a predominantly racial characteristic on the part of the Negroes." However, he made it clear that all this talk about "rights" should only occur after African Americans learned "responsibility." In the conclusion, Reamey voiced the concern of many white people in America concerning forced integration: creating the potential for teenage sexual immorality. "But until the moral standards of the whites and Negroes as groups," he asserted, "are brought much nearer the same level than now exists, we unhesitatingly affirm that any attempt to bring impressionable teen-agers together, not only in the classrooms and churches but at socials and parties and in camps and at picture-shows will be fraught with the greatest danger!" Although Reamey was unwilling to claim that all male African Americans were beasts, he used the image of uncontrollable black men with insatiable sexual appetites to warn his readers about the dangers of integration in the schools and by extension the churches, playing upon one of white southerners' biggest fears—miscegenation.[19]

Aubrey Brown experienced the power of white fears about race mixing in 1960. In a handwritten note to Brown that included the picture and article from the *Richmond News Leader* of a young black man and a young white woman on a date in New York, a woman from Grace Covenant Presbyterian (Richmond) inquired about the amount of space devoted in the *Presbyterian Outlook* to the integration cause and challenged Aubrey Brown to reconsider his position. "While waiting for our circle meeting to begin last Tuesday night at Grace Covenant," the writer stated, "I happened to glance through your recent issue of the Outlook. The space allotted to the fostering of integration was noticeable. Any person in the south who thinks realistically, knows full well that the integration of the negro and white races will inevitably mean the integration of blood." In a note of contempt, she added, "If this is what you want for your sons and daughters, you are on the right track."[20]

As the woman's message pointed out, southern white fears of interracial sexual contact, compounded by the feeling of intrusion by the federal government through the US Supreme Court, stood as a barrier to any argument about Christian duty to desegregation. The Christian claim to love one's neighbor competed equally with the Christian claim, at least in the public South, to puritanical sexual standards, which included no "race mixing." Reamey, like his "secular" counterpart at the *Richmond News Leader*, relied on that tension and exploited the statistics to bolster his case. As one letter to the editor in the *Virginia Methodist Advocate* pointed out, Reamey used the Bureau's statistics without noting that the Bureau still used the Jim Crow standard for defining who was "Negro." There would have been no way to know the number of illegitimate births from interracial couples. "If you want to be fair and honest," the writer charged, "investigate and publish your findings regarding the recent scandal involving white men and a fourteen year old Martinsville Negro girl."[21] It was one of many responses to Reamey's editorial in the weeks and months that followed. To his credit, he does not appear to have hampered debate within the *Virginia Methodist Advocate* because he published such different opinions.

The publication of the editorial created a firestorm among

Virginia Methodists. For most of the 1950s, no other article or editorial garnered as much attention.[22] While a substantial number of the letters supported Reamey's position, Virginia Methodist pastors took issue with the editor of Virginia Methodists' "official organ" propagating segregationist rhetoric. Reamey's use of statistics alone outraged a number of subscribers because it called into question the moral integrity of black people. It also appeared to fly in the face of the love ethic commanded in the gospel. Yet the republication of David Lawrence's editorial from *US News & World Report*, one month after Reamey's "Moral Standards" editorial, exposed the growing rift between desegregation supporters and opponents within the Virginia Methodist Conference.[23]

In the editorial, Lawrence argued that the people of Arkansas had spoken clearly on the issue of desegregation by reelecting Governor Orval Faubus to a third term by a wide margin. The thesis of the op-ed piece revolved around a doctrinaire belief in "States' Rights." After acknowledging that he personally had nothing against integration, Lawrence concluded, "The people of every State, however, are entitled to their right of self-government. If it was intended by the Constitution that there be uniformity of law throughout the States, then logically the Supreme Court long ago should have declared invalid all those laws which vary from State to State in different fields of human relations."[24] The publication of the editorial also indicated a shift in Reamey's editorial tactics. Up to this point, he tried to maintain at least the semblance of fairness in the debate. With the publication of this piece in a religious periodical, however, Reamey bared his segregationist soul and revealed an openly defiant spirit to desegregation.

J. William Hough, a Methodist pastor in Fairfax, responded to the Lawrence editorial with righteous indignation. Objecting that Lawrence told only part of the story in Little Rock—the school board had worked for sometime to integrate schools and Faubus made the first extreme move by sending in armed Guardsmen—the pastor took exception to Lawrence's interpretation of events in Arkansas. Hough wrote: "In supposedly voting for States Rights, they [the people of Arkansas] have endorsed a flagrant misuse of the authority of the Governor. In so doing they have encouraged Governor Faubus to continue to misuse his authority. And in so doing they have given encouragement to other individuals and groups who are seeking to defy the Supreme Court on the erroneous basis that States Rights are superior to the rights of individual citizens."[25] Hough then turned his attention to Reamey's use of the editorial. Claiming that Reamey's publication of the op-ed piece "implied endorsement" on the part of the *Virginia Methodist Advocate*, he believed that Reamey now had "given . . . tacit endorsement to the 'Massive Resistance' of the Supreme Court." Hough recounted the litany of public statements made from the General Conference and the Council of Bishops to the Virginia Conference's recent actions regarding support for the *Brown* decision. According to the pastor from Fairfax, the Methodist editor had overstepped his authority by publishing a position contrary to the Methodist Church's stance, particularly one that came directly from the editor himself. Ending his letter, Hough suggested that the "deepest tragedy" in the South was that the "wrong people" made the most noise and that honest Christians could not stand for such injustice. "I do not believe," he lamented, "that the majority of Christians—Methodist or otherwise—in the South are in favor of enforced segregation and its foundation concept that Negroes are inferior to others."[26]

With his editorial authority challenged, Reamey struck back in the same issue with an editorial directed at Hough's objections. He began by claiming that Hough had missed Lawrence's main point about states' rights because of Hough's inflated sense of race, a position that typically surrounds discussions of racial oppression. Reamey commented that the issue of "integration" was tangential to states' rights. The argument, similar to Kilpatrick's own position, involved Reamey's prioritizing of issues. Before any conversation about desegregation, he thought, states had to establish constitutional authority. Both Kilpatrick and Reamey attempted to argue that race was a tangential issue. As a sign of his belief that this debate was not about race, Reamey defended his editorial position by stating that an editor must present both sides of any argument, even an opinion that might offend. He chose Lawrence's piece because "Mr. Lawrence's editorial, in our opinion, gave one of the sanest interpretations we have anywhere seen of the issues he happened to be discussing." Since Reamey saw this as a states' rights issue, he dismissed Hough's claim that publishing the piece endorsed massive resistance. If the tone of Reamey's editorial had not put to rest any question about his allegiance to segregation, his conclusion did. "With reference to the Conference (Virginia) resolution 'which would deny the use of church facilities' if public schools are closed," the editor wrote, "let it be said the action was purely advisory. Every local Methodist church is free to decide for itself what action to take should the occasion arise"[27]—the same position Bishop Garber explained in the *Life* round-table discussion.[28] The final observation reversed Reamey's dogged attack on the massive resistance laws in 1956. The state cannot force public money to run parochial schools but churches themselves could choose to open such schools and should feel free to do so.

While some supported Reamey's use of the Lawrence editorial, several ministers took exception to the Methodist editor's use of editorial space to object to Hough's letter.[29] J. W. Reynolds Jr., a Methodist pastor who spent a few years in the mid-1950s pastoring a church in Richmond, wrote a letter calling into question Reamey's editorial judgment in the face of such blatant disregard for the Methodist church's *Discipline*, which affirmed the need for integrating society and the instruction for all Methodist churches to work for the end of Jim Crow laws both inside and outside the church. "Certainly your spirit in the July 10 editorial ['Integration and Moral Standards']," Reynolds claimed, "coupled with the publication of the Lawrence article a month later, and earlier editorials, builds up the case for one to deduct that your editorial position differs radically in spirit from the stand of The Methodist Church on the removal of racial discrimination." Then he used an economic threat similar to one used by Reamey regarding a letter from an individual at a Virginia Conference institution who disagreed with his stance.[30] Reynolds stated that Reamey should not in good, clear conscience ask for help from Virginia pastors to sell his magazine when he refused to uphold the spirit and letter of the church's *Discipline*. "If you insist on doing so," he asserted, "then I submit that you forfeit your right to call upon us pastors to sell your publication in our congregations on the basis that it makes good Methodists of them!"[31] Reynolds's complaint highlighted the double-edged problem for Virginia Methodists. As noted earlier, Bishop Garber defended the Methodist tradition of individual conscience having final say over such social matters as racism in the church. As much as Garber claimed "individual conscience," the southern Methodist denomination had given Garber wiggle room on desegregation. The General Conference only passed a "resolution" printed in the *Discipline* regarding race, which had little binding effect except on the conscience. The *Discipline* is the ruling constitutional authority for Methodists. But the resolutions, which were printed in the *Discipline*, were not part of church law, and therefore, held no binding effect on bishops, pastors, or congregations. Yet what happened to the Virginia Conference when the bishop and his editor held a position different from his charges?

The ministers of the Richmond District thought Reamey's position on desegregation egregious enough that they petitioned the editor to have the *Virginia Methodist Advocate* publish the *Discipline's* statement on "The Methodists and Race."[32] At their monthly gathering in September (1958), Dr. J. Callaway Robertson, pastor of Christ Church, read the resolution. Without noting the vote count, the *Virginia Methodist Advocate* reported that the motion carried. Included with the report of the Richmond District meeting, the *Virginia Methodist Advocate* published the General Conference's resolution on race and proposed six steps for alleviating racial discrimination. Among the six steps cited by the Conference, the Richmond Methodist ministers meant for the readers of the *Virginia Methodist Advocate* to understand two important issues. The first involved the way the General Conference held Methodist institutions, including churches and "publishing agencies," as needing to be above racial discrimination. How could the Virginia Conference's hierarchy stand in opposition to the General Conference's resolution on race, the Richmond ministers wondered? The second concern addressed by the *Discipline* encouraged "bishops, district superintendents, pastors, and lay leaders" to work for better relations at the national, state, and local level with the Central Jurisdiction (the separate black connectional body within the framework of the Methodist denomination).[33] Though the thrust of the resolution encouraged reflection on the part of the individual and left open room for multiple interpretations of the text, the Richmond District ministers wanted the bishop and editor to adhere to the spirit of the proclamation.

Not wanting the national body to be their sole source of authority, the ministers also asked that the motion passed at the previous Virginia Annual Conference regarding the use of Methodist buildings for private schools be published. The motion declared, "The Virginia Annual Conference of The Methodist Church, in regular session assembled, is opposed to the use of Methodist Church property to house any part of or substitute for the state school system in the event the public schools are closed." Quoting from its June 19, 1958, comment on the motion, the *Virginia Methodist Advocate* noted that the resolution "simply 'recommends' to the local church and has no binding power."[34] This final statement in the article about the Richmond district ministers' petition to publish a *Discipline* resolution, along with the editorial reaction to Hough, presented the *Virginia Methodist Advocate* position and created the most compelling link between the opinion of Bishop Garber and the editorial position of Reamey.[35]

Several weeks after the article about the ministers' meeting, the *Virginia Methodist Advocate* published an editorial displaying little sensitivity to the month-long debate over Virginia Methodists and desegregation or the spirit of both the resolution on race found in the church's *Discipline* and the vote of the Virginia Conference. Under the title "Why Not a Boys' School at Blackstone?," Reamey encouraged readers to think about the possibility of turning a little-used denominational retreat center in Virginia's Southside into a private school that served as a feeder school to Virginia Methodists' school in Front Royal, Randolph-Macon Academy.[36] The Richmond ministers had their answer to the Virginia Conference hierarchy's public position on desegregation. Reamey would continue to publish his segregationist opinions and Bishop Garber would respond publicly with indifference. The purpose of the Richmond district ministers' call to accountability could be obscured by the lack of change in the paper's editorial policy. This was yet another example of how a public pronouncement meant little in terms of concrete action.

Yet that interpretation, similar to the interpretation given by Numan Bartley concerning the RMA's statement on race, tells only part of the story. The Richmond district ministers, not unlike their counterparts in the Richmond Ministers' Association, held a standard contrary to "official" positions taken by those in power. In effect, the ministers said to their bishop that they could no longer support the mission of the official "organ" of the denomination. More importantly, they created an alternate understanding of the gospel message from the one Virginia Methodists received from their paper. To his credit, Reamey aired their contrary views and created an atmosphere of open debate concerning race within the *Virginia Methodist Advocate*. But the debate also revealed the limits of priestly authority. While Garber held final say within the confines of his conference, Richmond Methodist pastors called attention to the discrepancy between their bishop and the position of the General Conference. Garber could choose to punish his wayward charges and risk upsetting the life of both the Annual and Virginia Conferences, or publically appear neutral and maintain some sense of order within his jurisdiction. By choosing the latter, Garber allowed Reamey to continue to publish segregationist rhetoric while at the same time allowing his desegregationist pastors to speak their minds. Though the published voice of the Virginia Conference held firm segregationist ideas, Virginia Methodist pastors had the opportunity to address the desegregation crisis with prophetic convictions. So who spoke for Virginia Methodists? In theory, the Virginia Conference, but in practice, both sides spoke to Virginia Methodists, while their contradictory impulses showed why limited concerted action could take place.

Richmond Presbyterians: Limits of Prophetic Impulses

Presbyterians courted a predominately middle-class constituency in Richmond as elsewhere. When looking to start a "Negro" congregation in Richmond in the late 1940s and early 1950s, East Hanover Presbytery canvassed neighborhoods of black middle-class residents. The result created All Souls Presbyterian and as the neighborhood demographic shift occurred in Barton Heights, it allowed Overbrook Presbyterian to move westward. Both sessions belonged to East Hanover. This strategy of separation had its roots in Richmond Presbyterian life. Andrew Murray noted in his history of Presbyterian work with black people that as early as 1866 white Richmond Presbyterians had struggled to reach out to newly freed slaves. With the Presbyterian "formal" worship style, requiring a "certain amount of sophistication," Richmond Presbyterians counted few black people among their numbers by 1889. When a northern Presbyterian "missionary" began work with black people in Richmond, he started with a nucleus of two. Less than ten years later, the community had grown to fifty-eight.[37] What remains unclear is what happened to this congregation. There is little evidence that directly connects this group with the outreach mission at Seventeenth Street, East Hanover Presbytery's identified starting point of its ministry with African Americans.

The Seventeenth Street "church," however, sheds light on Richmond Presbyterians' emerging status as a prophetic voice in southern Presbyterian life. In 1898, the Presbyterian seminary at Hampden-Sydney in Farmville, Virginia, moved to Richmond. With the move, Union Theological Seminary began to train ministers of the gospel in an urban context.[38] By the 1910s, students at Union connected the promise of the gospel message to the social ills around them, including racism. Seventeenth Street mission did not attract middle-class black people but labored in Richmond's poorest section, known as Shockhoe Bottom. The faculty had begun to apply modern scholarship to biblical studies and encouraged an ethical component to ministerial life. With the emergence of higher criticism and the social gospel in theological education, professors at Union created a fertile breeding ground for progressive theological thinking within East Hanover Presbytery. Though the process took some time, the effects of Union were felt in Richmond and southern Presbyterian life as young ministers began to call into question the strict adherence to a Calvinism that spoke eloquently about God's demanding justice but said little about God's mercy within oppression social systems. By 1935, East Hanover Presbytery published a report that "called attention to some of the more extreme statements [about] the Confession [of Faith]."[39] In a move designed to revise the Confession of Faith—the defining statement of doctrine and practice—for the southern Presbyterian Church, the presbytery created space for discussion at the synod and General Assembly levels by having the presbytery acknowledge the archaic language of the confession. The vigorous debate that followed showed how southern Presbyterianism was trying to move away from "rigid Calvinism," with East Hanover Presbytery leading the way.[40] Even though all of the changes advocated by East Hanover did not come to pass, the discussion and minor changes showed East Hanover's capacity to lead the way for the larger denominational body by taking a progressive stand.

Richmond Presbyterians took significant leadership in the area of race relations. With individuals like Elinor Curry, Aubrey Brown, E. T. Thompson, John Marion; newly ordained pastors like Sherwood McKee; and the presence of Union Theological Seminary and Presbyterian School of Christian Education, East Hanover Presbytery encouraged discussions regarding its churches and race in the middle part of the twentieth century.[41] The presbytery went beyond mouthing simple lip service to race relations by founding two African American congregations and allowing a racially mixed congregation in Barton Heights to hire a black pastor.[42] The inclusion of African American congregations would put pressure on East Hanover Presbytery to find ways to include African Americans in their affairs, particularly at the denominational level. Unlike the other Protestant denominational bodies in Richmond, East Hanover Presbytery did not set up a separate structure for black congregations. Union Theological Seminary accepted its first full-time black graduate student in the early 1950s and its first full-time African American seminarian as a resident in 1956.[43] Unlike the other white denominations in Richmond, Presbyterians had the leadership, institutions, and resources to bring about the greatest difference in race relations among white Presbyterian churchgoers.

The national and state Presbyterian bodies had held strong positions against racial discrimination and segregation as early as the late 1940s. By 1953, the Synod of Virginia had integrated Massanetta, a retreat center for the synod, for such official church business as presbytery and synod gatherings.[44] As one observer noted, if the Virginia Synod wanted to know how churches would respond to a church court opinion, the East Hanover Presbytery would weigh in first on the matter and the synod would usually follow suit.[45] However, the presbytery was not conflict-free when it came to the issue of race. For example, in 1956 a resolution from a Richmond pastor asking the presbytery to take a position on race relations received a less-than-heroic response when the chairman of the Committee on Christian Relations stated that the General Assembly and the synod had made adequate statements on that issue and received no further redress.[46]

John Bright, the internationally esteemed professor of the Old Testament at Union Theological Seminary in Virginia, chaired East Hanover's Committee on Christian Relations (which until 1947 had been the Moral and Social Welfare Committee) at the time of the resolution request. As the head of this committee, Bright had control over the response to the resolution calling on the presbytery to address the pressing issues concerning race and Virginia's General Assembly in 1956. His reluctance to issue another resolution showed how Richmond Presbyterians could look prophetic against the backdrop of massive resistance but struggled internally with how to respond. Bright, who came to Union in 1940 after receiving his PhD from Johns Hopkins University, represented Union's progressive move toward higher criticism, particularly as it related to the first five books of the Old Testament. His scholarly pursuit was tempered by a strong sense of commitment to the Presbyterian tradition. As Ernest T. Thompson noted in his history of southern

Presbyterians, John Bright attempted to provide "an evangelical and Bible-centered theology" that refused to cater to "ultra-fundamentalism and certainly not radical liberalism," but "preserve[d] the virtues and avoid[ed] the excesses of both."[47] This theological tendency found expression in his social commitments.

In a letter to Aubrey Brown, Bright articulated a complicated position regarding public stances against desegregation. The letter, dated shortly after the RMA's publication of the Statement of Conviction, appeared to be addressing Aubrey Brown's concern that he, Bright, had not publicly stood with the RMA. Bright's name did not appear in the *Richmond Times-Dispatch* survey, although he mentioned to Brown in the letter that he had been out of town during that time. In response to Aubrey Brown's inquiry, he wrote: "Yes I did tell how the prophets said their say in the face of rough situations. And so ought I as a preacher of the gospel. If I ever fail to do so, or pull the punches, to whatever degree I have done so, that is sin—no less."[48] However, after admitting that a minister of the gospel has a duty to speak against injustice, he chastised Brown's contention that resolutions speak prophetically. "But I do not recall," Bright admonished, "any case where prophets achieved their ends by signing resolutions. Which may prove that there are other ways." He recounted how Union had been desegregated not by public proclamations but by quietly exercising a private institution's right to govern itself. Noting his own use of higher criticism, Bright stated, "Had there been manifestos on the subject of freedom on critical issues we would never have got on so fast." He did not offer a solution for how a prophet knew when to speak. While acknowledging that there were times to be counted, Bright believed that ministers should not fabricate those times. In a move resembling his position on higher criticism, he wrote, "Most often my vote is a Yes and No. If that makes me wishy-washy, so be it. . . . I see to [*sic*] many pale grays in the midst of blacks and whites."[49] Bright assumed a fairly progressive position on race by his positive acceptance of black students as equal partners in theological education. But he lamented the public nature of resolutions. Brown appeared to be calling Bright's hand, but the Old Testament professor saw no contradiction between his teaching about the prophets and his refusal to act like a "prophet" for Aubrey Brown. The correspondence from John Bright to Aubrey Brown, both dedicated Presbyterians, showed how a single concerted action by any religious organization was hampered by individual preferences, even when two individuals saw a social issue like desegregation as a positive good. The prophetic impulse of the heart did not always translate to a public call for broader social action.

Bright agreed with Aubrey Brown that segregation was morally corrupt but could not agree with him on how to respond to the pressing social issue. The separation was by degree. What happened, however, when Richmond Presbyterians disagreed over desegregation? The most vexing problem for Richmond Presbyterians was the battle to desegregate their newly created summer camp facility north of Richmond in Hanover County. The presbytery established Camp Hanover in 1957 as a summer camp for junior and senior high school students who were members of the presbytery's congregations. The presbytery minutes for the early 1957 meetings appear vague on what integrating the camp might mean for the presbytery. Except for some procedural issues and the announcement of camp's director John E. Ensign, the minutes provide few details about the structure of the camp's summer programs.

Following the presbytery's vote in spring 1957 to open the camp on an integrated basis, the session at First Presbyterian, Richmond, called on the presbytery to explain the possibility of a "fully integrated" camp. In particular, the members of the session wanted to know whether segregated living and dining arrangements had been made for each period of the camp. In blunt terms they asked, "Is it intended that the negro children be housed in separate tents or cabins from the white children, or will the two races be mixed in the same housing facility?"[50] The response from Ensign and from the clerk of the presbytery impressed no one on First Presbyterian's session and that body addressed the issue once again through a letter written to the clerk in the fall of 1957. However, by that time the camp had operated one full summer schedule and at least two of the two-week (senior high) camps were completely integrated—black and white children living together in the same tents/cabins and eating together. It was one thing to form a black Presbyterian congregation and provide some financial means for its success. However, it was an entirely different matter to have white children sleeping and changing clothes in the same tents or cabins with black children.

The struggle over desegregated high school camp continued at presbytery meetings for the remainder of fall 1957 and into the following spring over the nature of integration at Camp Hanover. Since the presbytery had previously left the matter of integration to the discretion of the camp director, some churches in the presbytery asked whether camp sessions integrated on a full basis, that is, with shared sleeping quarters and dining arrangements. By May 1958, First Presbyterian had "overtured"—the process in Presbyterian rules to redress an issue of the presbytery—the East Hanover Presbytery to reconsider its previous stance. This formal request by a church session provided congregations with a formal procedure to address church policy or doctrine. With the support of eleven other congregations, the petition requested that the presbytery "discontinue immediately the policy of integration of the white and Negro races at Camp Hanover, except in groups engaged in the transaction of official business of the churches."[51]

Camp Hanover became a "test case" over denominational policy for both social progressives and conservatives within the presbytery. Progressives had found a way to partially integrate an aspect of presbytery life and wanted to prove that young people could mingle in a proper Christian context without the world coming to an end. Conservatives had found what they thought was the breach in the presbytery's fairly progressive social agenda and wanted to stop the flood before it overflowed its banks. The struggle over Camp Hanover revealed a great deal about how denominational polity played a role in religious positions taken with regard to racial issues.[52]

In Presbyterian polity, the local church, or session, governs its members through a body known as "elders," with the pastor acting as a moderator. Moving out from the local church, churches in a defined geographical location form a network of cooperating bodies known as a presbytery. The presbytery examines, ordains, and installs ministers, reviews reports from sessions in its geographical boundaries, and provides a forum for complaints by churches in the presbytery. Presbyteries join together to form a synod. The national body that governs matters pertaining to doctrine and discipline is the General Assembly. A complaint can move from the session level to the General Assembly but only after being heard by the presbytery and then the synod courts. Lay members provide leadership at the local level as elders in their congregations. Lay leaders can hold an enormous amount of influence when a minister is not present. Second Presbyterian, Richmond, which had not joined First Presbyterian, Richmond, in the previous overtures, was without a pastor in 1959 when they joined First Richmond in petitioning the presbytery to end integration at Camp Hanover.[53] In the case of Camp Hanover, one minister and one lay delegate from each church session voted on the measure. Since an overwhelming majority of sessions voted for the desegregation of Camp Hanover, the desegregation agenda of the presbytery's clergy could move forward. This denominational structure placed a significant burden on anyone who wanted to stem the progressive social agenda within the presbytery, synod, or General Assembly on desegregating denominational life.

As early as 1954, the General Assembly of the Presbyterian Church in the United States (PCUS) articulated a position through its committee on social ministries that denounced segregation in any form in Presbyterian churches, retreat centers, and colleges. The Synod of Virginia had already integrated its retreat center, Massanetta, in all official business of the churches. So, in 1958 when First Richmond and the other ten congregations petitioned the Hanover Presbytery (the presbytery had changed its name from East Hanover) to reconsider its decision to integrate Camp Hanover for its summer programs, they faced a rather substantial obstacle. Not only had the presbytery already spoken on the matter, the synod and General Assembly had indicated their willingness to support an active agenda to integrate Presbyterian life. A local congregation could voice opposition, but a simple majority ruled in the presbytery. And in the Hanover Presbytery that meant an integrated summer camp for members of the presbytery's churches.

The overture drew a distinction between "official" adult contact and casual youth contact. Apparently, they conceded that with the inclusion of black congregations and black pastors in the presbytery official business of the church could not be conducted with such restrictive codes. However, the supporters of the overture believed that intimate social relations between black children and white children were not the business of the presbytery. As the letter from the session at First Richmond had asserted in the fall of 1957, "our church is not integrated, yet the children of our members, if they attend, are faced with the possibility of integration."[54] It was clear from these statements that some in Hanover Presbytery lacked any zeal for the presbytery's progressive social agenda regarding race and children. Close physical contact between young people of different races worried many white Presbyterians in the Richmond area. Since many southern white people opposed integrated classrooms because of the possible contact among boys and girls, particularly black boys and white girls, the overture's supporters wondered if the presbytery had begun to endorse intimate black–white relations.

Conservative theology, however, did not necessarily predispose a person to conservative racial practices. At the May 27, 1958, presbytery meeting, West End Presbyterian (Hopewell, Virginia) counteroverture the presbytery to follow its current desegregated course at Camp Hanover. William Todd has noted that the pastor, William E. Hill Jr., was known in presbytery circles for his "conservative theology." And yet the overture from West End affirmed the prophetic stand made by the presbytery. The session's statement read, "Respectfully overtures Hanover Presbytery to continue the present policy at Camp Hanover and that the presbytery call upon all faithful followers of the Lord Jesus Christ to try to forget their differences and cooperate together in the work of the church. The interests of the Kingdom are too large and the issues too great for us to quibble over things which will seem to the next generation quite insignificant."[55] In fact, it could be argued that Hill's position on Camp Hanover came from the same theological source as Aubrey Brown's: an emphasis on "Kingdom work." Hill and West End Presbyterian wanted to move beyond segregation because the cause of the Kingdom appeared greater than the squabble over black and white children camping together. Brown believed that a Christian should see another Christian as brother or sister without regard for skin color **and** be willing to practice that belief by sharing in personal contact. Both approaches reached the same conclusion, even if their specific motives were different. The presbytery affirmed its earlier position regarding full integration at Camp Hanover by a vote of 61 to 40.[56]

The internal debate over desegregating the presbytery's summer camp unveiled a growing rift among Richmond Presbyterians about desegregation. Not everyone in East Hanover Presbytery was ready for desegregation, particularly as it related to their own children and mixed living arrangements at the camp. Denominational polity had dictated the move to desegregate by the presbytery. The overture process allowed opposition voices to ask the presbytery to rethink its position; however, segregation voices could not sway the majority of the presbytery, which was dominated by progressive-minded pastors on race, to change its position. The closeness of the vote showed how divided Presbyterians could be on desegregation. Hanover Presbytery's progressive stance regarding race marked it as prophetic in light of massive resistance, but internal dissension showed the limits of that voice. The presbytery's public position almost always placed it on the prophetic end of the continuum; however, individual congregations could adapt their strategies to maintain the status quo. Few African Americans in Richmond actively searched for Presbyterian communities of faith, so congregations had little to fear in the desegregation of their pews. And if the presbytery's position offended an individual's racial sensibilities with its action regarding Camp Hanover, parents could keep their children at home. The will of the presbytery did not necessarily affect the hearts of the people in its pews.

As Richmond Presbyterians and Methodists debated the merits of self-desegregation, the massive resistance train derailed itself everywhere in Virginia except Prince Edward County. Curiously, Kilpatrick had laid the groundwork for the end of the defense of massive resistance a little over four months after his stand for closing Richmond schools. His sudden shift defies clear explanation. However, Kilpatrick, as a pragmatist, saw the handwriting on the wall when every legal means Virginia put toward segregation failed to pass constitutional muster. Massive resistance's consistent legal defeats in both the state and federal courts encouraged all but the most ardent segregationists (read: Prince Edward County) to abandon the resistance strategy. In his editorial retreat from massive resistance at all cost, Kilpatrick signaled a hope that a provision of the Gray Plan, which he helped destroy, could be resurrected and that limited (read: "token") desegregation could occur in localities that were ready. Virginius Dabney, editor of the *Richmond Times-Dispatch*, followed that call the next day in his own editorial. Moderating forces, determined to save free public education for white children, had captured momentum from general discontent over school closings and started to organize, founding local chapters of the "Committee for Public Schools" all over the state. This "moderate" movement grabbed the rhetorical center in the public debate from the massive resistance forces. With a wavering governor, backpedaling editors, and energized public school supporters showing signs of massive resistance's defeat in late 1958, the Virginia State Supreme Court rendered the school closing laws of 1956 unconditional. By 1959 in Virginia, except in Prince Edward County, massive resistance was dead. Without the fanfare of Little Rock, black school children entered the previously "white" Chandler Middle School—in Barton Heights—for the first time as students in September 1960, and quietly desegregated Richmond public schools.[57]

EPILOGUE

Sitting from their offices in Washington, DC, NAACP lawyers watched in amazement with the rest of the nation as college students confronted the *private* world of the Jim Crow South.[1] As the legal team that had brought the United States the *Brown* cases continued to dismantle the public side of Jim Crow laws through equal access to schools, transportation, and parks, a group of college students in Greensboro, North Carolina, confronted the segregationists' heart by challenging equal access to private spaces. In the process, these young black students revealed how far they would go to challenge segregation.

The lunch counter sit-ins at the Greensboro, North Carolina, Woolworth's in early February 1960 were followed later in the month by similar protests in Richmond. The protesters, students from Virginia Union University (VUU), targeted downtown lunch counters at several department stores. As white church leaders were well aware, the largely unwritten segregation policy in churches presented the most glaring hypocrisy in American life. Students willing to cross the line in business settings where their arrests revealed no injustice in the law might be willing to expand their protest into other private spaces. In places like Memphis, the "kneel-in" campaign was part of this larger push for desegregated access in American life. In Richmond, however, students did not target churches, at least not in the early 1960s.

With more than 200 Virginia Union students participating, the "sit-downs," as newspaper accounts initially referred to these activities, struck at the core of black–white relations in the South.[2] For all the drama over public school desegregation, black citizens had for decades crossed Jim Crow's strict line of demarcation through retail exchanges. At its inception, Jim Crow's private lines were as demeaning as anything that occurred publicly. Black women were forced to buy clothing without trying it on in the store, and these women could not return the purchase if it failed to fit properly. Black customers were forced to use separate entrances into eateries; white owners were happy to take their money without acknowledging the indignity those shoppers were forced to accept. African Americans were restricted from sitting in certain areas of churches because of the color of their skin, so white congregations were free to assume no African Americans would sit next to them in the pews. Student protesters had decided it was worth confronting segregation on private property and in doing so exposed for white congregations the nature of their segregated churches.

From the start, the protests placed an unusual burden on segregationists like Kilpatrick. Editorializing in the wake of the first arrests at lunch counters in Richmond, the *Richmond News Leader* opined that the visual images of the protests did not bode well for white southerners. The point was true enough. "Many a Virginian must have felt a tinge of wry regret," the editorial noted, "at the state of things as they are, in reading of Saturday's 'sit-downs' by Negro students in Richmond stores. Here were the colored students, in coats, white shirts, ties, and one of them was reading Goethe and one taking notes from a biology text. And here, on the sidewalk outside, was a gang of white boys come to heckle, a ragtail rabble, slack-jawed, black-jacketed, grinning fit to kill, and some of them, God save the mark, were waving the proud and honored flag of the Southern States in the last war fought by gentlemen. *Eheu!* It gives one pause."[3] The remainder of the lengthy editorial focused on why the students did not have a constitutional right to eat at the stores. If Kilpatrick and others wanted to keep the discussion on constitutional rights, it was clear that neither the smartly dressed students inside nor the "rabble" outside were interested in that particular kind of framing of the issue. In this way, Kilpatrick's dispassionate defense of segregation no longer carried the day, if it ever did.

If the *Brown* decision felt like the book hitting Mrs. Turpin in the face in Flannery O'Connor's "Revelation," the student protests were more like the condemnation from Mary Grace when Mrs. Turpin expected an apology. It's not enough to have black students call segregation practices immoral. When white students joined the ranks of picketers, the pressure from within the fold grew greater. Within the first weeks of the protest movement in Richmond, students from Union Theological Seminary in Richmond joined the marches outside of two department stores, Thalhimer's and Miller & Rhoads.[4] In nightly meetings these students strategized with VUU students to keep pressure on the stores to end segregation at the lunch counters and in store practices themselves. Aubrey Brown III, following his father's dedication to the idea of a desegregated South, led Union students to participate in the boycott.[5] Earlier in his tenure at Union he played a key role in making students aware of how the issue of segregation within churches affected society. By 1960 John Marion, who Aubrey Brown III invited to campus to discuss segregation's moral quandary, had moved from Richmond to Nashville to carry on his ministry of racial reconciliation. In his place other young leaders were stepping forward, willing to go in directions that even Marion would not lead.

The Richmond Area Council on Human Relations also came to the aid of the student protestors. By early April, with the picket lines still going strong, the council passed a resolution calling on the store owners to end segregation practices in their facilities. The resolution framed the issue the same way the Richmond Ministers' Association (RMA) had three years earlier. "As citizens of the Richmond-Petersburg-Hopewell, Virginia, area," the statement read, "we take our stand in support of the requests of Negroes in our community to be treated with dignity that belongs to all men through our common creation and our democratic ideals." While acknowledging that not every demonstrator's intention might be pure or that the method was not ideal, the council's position was clear: "We support them to bear public witness to the fact that discrimination against any people on the basis of birth is in violation of our Judeo-Christian heritage and our democratic principles."[6] Aubrey Brown Jr.'s leadership in both the Virginia Council on Human Relations and its Richmond chapter placed him at a critical juncture for conversations about race and religion in Richmond and throughout Virginia. He played important roles in shaping how the Richmond Presbyterians and Presbyterians throughout the region responded to a desegregated order, participating ultimately on the US Commission on Civil Rights from the mid-1960s into the 1970s.

Brown expected others to see the logic in his argument for a desegregated South the same way he did, particularly as students were willing to expose segregation for the hypocrisy it was. Like Kilpatrick, however, Brown failed to see that others would react to spectacles of protest in a different manner. Having debated John Bright over the use of resolutions when the RMA spoke against the massive resistance laws, he should have anticipated growing institutional concern by Union Theological Seminary administrators and trustees over the activities of its students in the protests. In a letter sent to his brother James, written the evening after a faculty meeting at Union, Brown expressed pain that administration officials would denounce the use of boycott tactics and required faculty to abstain from them. He appeared even more at a loss that faculty resigned themselves to the order. Brown's frustration was so great that he wrote a lengthy appeal to the faculty, calling on them to muster strength to fight for the cause of justice and equality.[7]

Though Aubrey Brown Jr. would continue to champion the cause of a desegregated church in a desegregated society, his mission continually rubbed up against competing claims of what the role of the church should be in the struggle. Richmond hosted no fewer than four conferences on race and religion in the 1960s, with Brown at the center of almost of them. In 1966, during the most extensive attempt to get churches talking about their role in maintaining segregation, the VCHR hosted a region-wide Conference on Race and Religion. Under Brown's leadership, the council held a plenary session with black and white ministers and civic leaders to engage in discussions over the role religious people could play in bringing about change. As it had from the beginning, the council included Catholic and Jewish participants, which in the heady days of the ongoing Second Vatican Council gave greater credibility to ecumenical work. George Reamey, however, took exception to the meeting and its apparent agenda. In a fairly long letter to Brown, Reamey wrote about his frustration that issues (from housing problems to economic justice) that he saw as unrelated to race often got connected to race anyway in public discourse. He chided Brown for wasting an opportunity to bring about real and substantive change by forcing folks to accept the "integrationist" agenda. Reamey ended the letter by noting that if another meeting were to be held in the future, "I suggest that something that appears to me to be a much more balanced kind of discussion could be scheduled."[8]

Brown's curt reply revealed two important issues for white church leaders during the desegregation period. Though he chastised Reamey for hearing only what he wanted to hear at the meeting, Brown's biggest criticism cut to Reamey's failure to notice his own disagreement with the Methodist Church's "official position" on desegregation. Brown noted that the VCHR's position was "not as far along as your church in its official support and authorizations."[9] The response, however, also showed the limits of creating a unified voice from white churches regarding desegregation. Neither man addressed the others' concern and appeared to talk past one another. If Brown's witness was prophetic, Reamey continued to find ways to mold his previous understanding of a segregated order within the changes of the mid-1960s. He participated in the conference after all, something he would not have done in the 1950s.

The sit-ins changed both the nature of the movement and the terms under which white leaders could control the discussion, particularly within church structures. The student protests of the 1960s, for all the good they did to reveal the continued trauma of segregation and why slow progress meant little change, also hardened positions of resistance at the level of private life. For every

Aubrey Brown in the church working to bring about dramatic and lasting change within churches there was a George Reamey looking for ways to justify life as it was. Even if Weatherford Memorial Baptist Church opened its doors on a desegregated basis in 1960, there were numerous churches working hard to keep their sanctuaries segregated. We know more about the latter than we do about the former. The different approaches to desegregation suggest that we have more ground to cover before we fully understand how white church leaders and white churches engaged the civil rights movement.

ACKNOWLEDGMENTS

This project grew out of a series of questions I formulated as a youth and young adult while still attending East Highland Park Baptist Church, located just across the border northeast of the city of Richmond in Henrico County. A mostly growing middle-class neighborhood formed in the 1930s and 1940s, the East Highland Park neighborhood became an example of an early wave of mid-twentieth century expansion out of the city. When I attended church in the 1970s and 1980s, the flight had already pushed farther north and my family was part of that movement away from the city. I am a product of busing desegregation orders in the 1970s and my relationships with African Americans in those schools made questions about racial categories and Christianity more pronounced as I grew older. The church taught me to love the "stranger," but as the neighborhood's demographic changed, the congregation struggled to make sense of the command in their own membership. I have learned that group formation and following Christ's dictum to love one's neighbor were not necessarily linked. The questions continue to animate my thinking about congregations and change.

What did it mean to learn to love the stranger while struggling to embrace a person who did not look like us? What does the gospel mean in a shifting social context? When I turned my attention to history as a profession, I knew I wanted to explore these questions on a scale larger than the congregation where I grew up. By limiting the study to a single city, I knew it would be easier to tease out the dynamics that play a role in congregational decisions on matters like desegregation. As I read newspaper accounts of how Richmond's ministerial leaders confronted the tactics of massive resistance, I shifted the focus off congregations to the larger question of school desegregation and its parallel challenge to congregational desegregation. Richmond became the place to start thinking about those questions.

I am equally grateful to East Highland Park Baptist Church because they helped to contribute to my sense of faith and how it is lived out. They encouraged and corrected my thinking in ways that resemble the process of book publication. In the course of this project, I have become indebted to many different kinds of communities. I will risk not mentioning many to call attention to a few who made the project enjoyable and in many ways better because of their encounter with the work. The librarians in the Albert and Shirley Small Special Collections Library at the University of Virginia always helped me track down the most remote pieces of the archives where Richmond and segregation/desegregation had a tag. The folks at the Virginia Historical Society also helped me cull obscure references in one archive that led me to more sources in their archives. Their generous handling of Aubrey Brown Jr.'s papers and the rich resources his family has left in their care stand as a testament to the important work that archives need to do to collect more ministers' papers. The archivist and reference librarians at Union Theological Seminary, Virginia Union University, Virginia Commonwealth University, and the University of Richmond patiently answered my queries and helped point me to other sources. While I cannot name them all individually, their guidance in this project made it a better book.

Archivists helped find sources, but more important to the reader of this volume are the people who read parts or the whole manuscript. It would not be in the form it is here without their critical reading and comments. Chief among those readers are Paul Harvey and Sarah Gardner. Paul encouraged the project almost from the beginning. His generous critiques generated more thinking on my part and clarified important moves in the argument. Sarah has read almost every word, twice, and continued to prompt me to put the work out for a broader audience. She helped me see that self-doubt limited my thinking on the subject. I had something important to say that needed to be said. I came to appreciate from both of them that a community of writing colleagues creates an environment where we test our ideas, and we hone those ideas in conversation with one another, not in isolation, which was mostly how I previously viewed the writing process. They both introduced me to the #GraftonLine Challenge, an online community of academic writers who provide encouragement. Posts about daily word counts helped me to think of the project as something done in small sections instead of a whole. I know only these two on the list but I watch every day as writers struggle with their own doubts and schedules to hammer out the things we call books and articles.

Others have read and commented on the manuscript. I will leave some of them out and for that omission I apologize. Those named had a significant hand in shaping some part of the current book. Heather Warren, Charles Marsh, and Wallace Best read early versions of the work and provided critical feedback resulting in the shape that it takes today. Art Remillard generously took on reading the introduction under a deadline and asked questions that I had not thought about, clarifying for me the weaknesses but also the strengths of the argument. Additionally, several years ago, I participated in a writing group at Mercer University in which we submitted writing samples and provided feedback to one another. Among that group, the leader, Bryan Whitfield, carefully and thoughtfully pushed me to think about how I conceptualized the larger project. The College of Liberal Arts' former dean Lake Lambert read short pieces of the manuscript and provided important financial support to get the project completed. Like all creations, we are protective of our writing even when we know its flaws. At every step of the way, I have watched caring people point out blind spots in my thinking and writing. For their patience and ability to see the project for what it could be, my debt remains great. This debt also extends to the editorial process with the University of Alabama Press. Their careful attention to the manuscript has made it better in form and thought.

At some point in the acknowledgments section of any book, writers thank their families. In my case it is not enough to thank them, though that is the most I can do here. During the time this book was coming into existence, my wife, Kerri, and I added three children to our household. My absence during critical times in our family's lives allowed me to finish but those absences also meant that Ethan, Evan, and Zoie did not have their dad around. As they grow older, they need me less, but it was important to me to be there for them. Thank you to the three of you for understanding—if not now, then hopefully in the future. My in-laws, Bryan and Sareta Shelburne, picked up the load helping Kerri with the children's busy schedules when I went to Richmond to do research. It is good to have cheerleaders in the house and next door.

I am also grateful for my mother's two sisters who sustained some part of this project. Lee Hanchey and her husband, Neal, allowed me to stay in their home near Richmond while I made archive runs late in the process. Wonderful food and conversations made archive work more enjoyable. Carol Kloster nudged from afar but gladly read an early draft of the manuscript and provided the most poignant moment of my research. After reading the chapter that discusses the desegregation of Camp Hanover in 1957, she told the story of how my grandfather (her father) drove his daughters out to the camp that summer only to learn about the desegregated sleeping and eating arrangements. He put the girls back in the car and drove home. It is a story I do not remember hearing while growing up within earshot of her mother. I assumed in the research that parents made individual choices about their children regardless of the denomination's position, but with this story, I had personal contact, even if remotely, to how that process worked. As is apparent, my family has as much to do with the book as archivists and colleagues. Their gentle prodding was helpful and their continuing well-wishes mean a great deal to me.

My mother and father nurtured my questioning nature. They both made it through high school and took some form of college-level classes, but they were part of a generation that often entered the workplace straight out of high school. Reaching adulthood in the greatest economic expansion in American history, they both did well and supported their only son. However, for them, sending me to college represented an opportunity for me to exceed their own dreams. My mother died ten years ago so she did not get to see this part of those dreams to completion. My dad's blindness will rob him of the chance to read the book himself. At heart my dad is a craftsman, a builder, so when I place a copy of the book in his hands he will understand what I do in words resembles what he built in homes. In both cases, their unconditional love for me gave me courage to see possibilities even when I doubted the reality.

My final thank you is for Kerri, to whom the book is dedicated. She saw the potential in this project, and me, long before I could. My absences were numerous, but my stubbornness in the writing process might have been harder on her than on me at times. I am slow in the task and doubt often paralyzed me. She knew I could complete the task and understood why it mattered. Her support and encouragement sustained me in ways that I will never be able to repay. I offer the dedication as a reminder to myself as much as her that without her presence this book would have never seen the light of day. Her guidance in big things and small make this journey worth every step.

NOTES

Introduction

1. I began my archival work for this project in the midst of the debate over where to place the monument. In some ways that debate has hovered around and through much of my thinking in what follows.

2. "Richmond Approves Monument to Ashe," *New York Times*, July 18, 1995, US Section. *http://www.nytimes.com/1995/07/18/us/richmond-approves-monument-to-ashe.html* (accessed August 21, 2015).

3. David Chappell, *Inside Agitators: White Southerners in the Civil Rights Struggle* (Baltimore: Johns Hopkins University Press, 1996); David Chappell, *Stone of Hope: Prophetic Religion and the Death of Jim Crow* (Chapel Hill: University of North Carolina Press, 1998); Stephen R. Haynes, *The Last Segregated Hour: The Memphis Kneel-Ins and the Campaign for Southern Church Desegregation* (New York: Oxford University Press, 2005); Carolyn Renee Dupont, *Mississippi Praying: Southern White Evangelicals and the Civil Rights Movement, 1945–1975* (New York: New York University Press, 2014); Joseph Reiff, *Born of Conviction: White Methodists and Mississippi's Closed Society* (New York: Oxford University Press, 2015).

4. Michael B. Chesson, *Richmond after the War: 1865–1890* (Richmond: Virginia State Library, 1981), 21–22.

5. Beth Barton Schweiger, *The Gospel Working Up: Progress and the Pulpit in Nineteenth-Century Virginia* (New York: Oxford University Press, 2000), chap. 6.

6. C. Vann Woodward, *The Strange Career of Jim Crow*, 2nd rev. ed. (New York: Oxford University Press, 1966), 6–7.

7. C. Vann Woodward, *Origins of the New South 1877–1913* (1951; Baton Rouge: Louisiana State University Press, 1971), 211–12; Charles E.

Wynes, *Race Relations in Virginia 1870–1902* (Charlottesville: University of Virginia Press, 1961), 39–50.

8. Samuel C. Shepherd Jr., *Avenues of Faith: Shaping the Urban Religious Culture of Richmond, Virginia, 1900–1929* (Tuscaloosa: University of Alabama Press, 2001), 5–6.

9. Chesson, *Richmond*, 172.

10. *Virginia State Constitution of 1902*, Section 31; Wynes, *Race Relations*, 66–67; Allen Moger, *Virginia: Bourbonism to Byrd 1870–1925* (Charlottesville: University of Virginia Press, 1968), 182–83, 190–91; Andrew Buni, *The Negro in Virginia Politics 1902–1965* (Charlottesville: University of Virginia Press, 1967), 20.

11. V. O. Key Jr. and Alexander Heard, *Southern Politics in State and Nation* (New York: A. A. Knopf, 1949), 19–35, particularly 25.

12. *Richmond News Leader*, February 15, 1951, 4.

13. Robert A. Pratt, *The Color of Their Skin: Education and Race in Richmond, Virginia 1954–1989* (Charlottesville: University of Virginia Press, 1992), 14–15.

14. Flannery O'Connor, "Revelation," in *Everything That Rises Must Converge* (1956; New York: Farrar, Straus and Giroux, 1998), 205–6.

15. There is a growing literature about how white Christians encountered the civil rights movement. Civil rights historiography ignored white Christian denominations' varied responses to the movement with the exceptions of a number of activists who wrote about their experiences. Will Campbell's early work on desegregation is an example of this type of writing. See Will D. Campbell, *Race and the Renewal of the Church* (Philadelphia: Westminster Press, 1962). David Chappell opened this line of inquiry in the late 1990s in *Inside Agitators* and *Stone of Hope*, which highlight the use of prophetic voices to undermine the Jim Crow system. Jonathan Bass, in *Blessed Are the Peacemakers: Martin Luther King Jr., Eight White Religious Leaders, and the "Letter from Birmingham Jail"* (Baton Rouge: Louisiana State University Press, 2001) gave us a nuanced treatment by examining the clergymen who are the addressees of Martin Luther King Jr.'s "Letter from Birmingham Jail." Carolyn Dupont (*Mississippi Praying*) and Stephen Haynes (*The Last Segregated Hour*) show how southern white Christians created various theological responses to civil rights challenges to southern social norms. *Born of Conviction*, Joe Reiff's look at southern Methodists, also suggests that we have not fully uncovered the layers of theological reflection and action carried out by white religious southerners. This project enters the conversation by looking at a place as much as a particular set of leaders or denominations. Richmond, Virginia, held a symbolic position in the American South, and religious leaders in the city were fully aware of this as some of them argued for a

desegregated society, including its religious institutions. Mechanisms—local, regional, and national—thwarted their success on a grand scale. Make no mistake, however, theses ministers did bring about change.

Chapter 1

1. John H. Marion Jr., "Magnificent Obsession: A Sermon Preached at Grace Covenant Presbyterian Church, Richmond, Virginia," Virginia Historical Society, General Collection, BX9178 M243 M2.

2. John Egerton, *Speak Now against the Day: The Generation before the Civil Rights Movement in the South* (Chapel Hill: University of North Carolina Press, 1995), 120–27.

3. John H. Marion Jr., "Farewell, My Lovely Magnolias," *Yale Review* XXXV, no. 3 (March 1946), 424.

4. Earlier in the decade, Marion had issued a challenge to use courtesy titles such as Miss, Mrs., or Mr. when discussing southern black people in the pages of *Christian Century*. He called the "southern fear" about racial change a "bugaboo." John H. Marion Jr. "Courtesy Across the Color Line," *Christian Century* LVII, no. 20 (May 15, 1940), 639.

5. "Discrimination Doomed, Say Presbyterians," *Richmond News Leader*, April 28, 1949, 1.

6. "Segregation's End Advocated By Churchman," *Richmond News Leader*, January 12, 1950, 5.

7. Marion, "Magnificent," 7 (emphasis added).

8. Gunnar Myrdal, *An American Dilemma: The Negro Problem and Modern Democracy* (New York: Harper & Row, 1962; originally published in 1944).

9. "Dr. Myrdal, Hurt, Can't Keep Two Richmond Dates," *Richmond News Leader*, May 12, 1954, 12A, column 3.

10. *Brown et al. v. Board of Education, Topeka et al.*, 98 L ed 873, 881. For the court's use of these psychological and sociological sources see page 881, note 11. In addition to Clark and Myrdal, the court included work done by E. Franklin Frazier.

11. "Transcendent Issue, II," editorial, *Richmond News Leader*, November 21, 1955, 10; the *Richmond News Leader* republished the series of editorials in pamphlet form in December for distribution.

12. Myrdal, *An American Dilemma*, 11. Even when Myrdal is not in use, the "ideal" church influences historians of the South. The dean of southern religious history Samuel S. Hill emphasizes that his history of the era, *Southern Churches in Crisis*, is important because it will allow churches to see where they went wrong. "A diagnosis," Hill stated, "of their illness is clearly a precondition of Christianity's regaining its rele-

vance for those to whom it seeks to minister." He concluded the paragraph with an impressive goal: "Through the use of historical and sociological tools, this study endeavors to provide the church with a richer and more *authentic* vision of itself and its mission" (emphasis added).

13. Myrdal, *An American Dilemma*, 10–11.

14. Ibid., 858, 862.

15. More recently, there have been two exceptional studies on white congregations and the attempt to keep white churches segregated. Stephen R. Haynes, *The Last Segregated Hour: The Memphis Kneel-Ins and the Campaign for Southern Church Desegregation* (New York: Oxford University Press, 2012) looks at the use of the kneel-in campaign to desegregate Second Presbyterian Church in Memphis, Tennessee. Carolyn Dupont, *Mississippi Praying: White Southern Christians and the Civil Rights Movement, 1945–1975* (New York: New York University Press, 2013) examines the way Christians in Mississippi deployed a theological understanding of segregation to maintain the practice in that state.

16. David Chappell, *Stone of Hope: Prophetic Religion and the Death of Jim Crow* (Chapel Hill: University of North Carolina Press, 1998).

17. Anthony P. Dunbar, "Fellowship of Southern Churchmen," in *Encyclopedia of Religion in the South*, Samuel S. Hill, ed. (Macon, GA: Mercer University Press, 1984), 252. Also see Anthony P. Dunbar, *Against the Grain: Southern Radicals and Prophets, 1929–1959* (Charlottesville: University of Virginia Press, 1981), 61.

18. Henry Lee Curry III, "The Confederate Careers of James Armstrong Duncan, Moses Drury Hoge, and Charles Frederic Ernes Minnigerode," PhD diss., Emory University, Atlanta, GA, 1971, 83–91.

19. David D. Ryan, *Four Days in 1865: The Fall of Richmond* (Richmond, VA: Cadmus Communications Corporation, 1993), 3–7; A. A. Hoehling and Mary Hoehling, *The Day Richmond Died* (New York: Madison Books, 1981), 113, 248; Virginius Dabney, *Richmond: The Story of a City*, rev. and expanded (1990; Charlottesville: University of Virginia Press, 1976), 189.

20. Egerton, *Speak Now*, 426.

21. "Dr. Johnson to Open, Close Interracial Church Parley," *Afro-American* (Richmond), March 2, 1946, 6.

22. "Unsegregated Church Plea of Conference Resolutions," *Afro-American* (Richmond), March 16, 1946, 1.

23. "Helping Dixie Find Its Soul," editorial, *Afro-American* (Richmond), March 16, 1946, 1–2. Since the *Afro-American* had its primary office in Baltimore, the paper allowed local editorials to appear on the front page.

24. Editorial, *Afro-American* (Richmond), March 16, 1946, 1–2.

25. Letter from John M. Ellison to Nelle Morton, March 22, 1946. The Fellowship of Southern Churchmen, Box 3, Folder 25, "March 21–27, 1946," Southern Collection, Wilson Library, University of North Carolina–Chapel Hill.

26. "Guideposts for Action," Fellowship of Southern Churchmen, Box 3, Folder 23, "Feb. 28–March 14, 1946," Southern Collection, Wilson Library, University of North Carolina–Chapel Hill.

27. Jane Dailey, *Before Jim Crow: The Politics of Race in Postemancipation Virginia* (Chapel Hill: University of North Carolina Press, 2000), 140–42.

28. "3 City Ministerial Groups Merge Into Inter-Racial Unit," *Richmond News Leader*, March 23, 1953, 20.

29. "Baptist Pastor Elected Head of Interracial Group Here," *Richmond News Leader*, April 27, 1953, 21.

30. Mayor Haddock and John Marion both had particularly good relationships with Francis Pickens Miller, a Charlottesville native.

31. "Protestant Ministers Pledge Segregation End," *Richmond News Leader*, November 30, 1953, 31.

32. *Richmond Times-Dispatch*, November 13, 1943, 4; November 21, 1943, Sec. IV, 2; Virginius Dabney, *Across the Years: Memories of a Virginian* (Garden City, NY: Doubleday, 1978), 391–96; Dabney republished the November 21 editorial in the appendix of his autobiography. Christopher Silver and John V. Moeser, *The Separate City: Black Communities in the Urban South, 1940–1968* (Lexington: University Press of Kentucky, 1995), 66.

33. Benjamin Muse, *Virginia's Massive Resistance* (Gloucester, MA: Peter Smith, 1969) 35–36; Robbins L. Gates, *The Making of Massive Resistance: Virginia's Politics of Public School Desegregation, 1954–1956* (Chapel Hill: University of North Carolina Press, 1964), 139–41.

34. Ernest T. Thompson, *Presbyterians in the South: 1890–1972* (Richmond, VA: John Knox Press, 1973), 534.

35. "Pastor Urges New Outlook on Race Ills," *Richmond News Leader*, December 28, 1953, 15; "Pastor Calls For 'Realistic' Race Attitude," *Richmond Times-Dispatch*, December 29, 1953, 1, 3.

36. Emile Durkheim, *The Elementary Forms of Religious Life*, trans. Karen E. Fields (New York: Free Press, 1995), 44. I am borrowing Karen Fields's understanding of Durkheim's phrase "moral communities" to emphasize the social nature of congregations as something other than "hodgepodges" of human groupings. Their "sacredness exists in the real, and its creation is the observable product of collective doing," xxxiv.

37. In this light, the Book of Ruth found in Hebrew scripture highlights the powerful way that priestly functions explain prophetic voices. Ruth

shows how Israel ends up with King David but in the process undermines the Levitical codes that forbid intermarriage with non-Hebrew tribes. In this way the text pushes back against the priestly injunctions that narrow the people's understanding of God's relationship with the people. God might be able to work with non-Jews.

38. Charles Marsh, *God's Long Summer: Stories of Faith and Civil Rights* (Princeton, NJ: Princeton University Press, 1997), 46–48, 79–81. Marsh's two chapters on Hamer and Bowers delineate their theological positions throughout the chapters, so I have chosen to cite the conclusions to the chapters. I am partial to Stephen R. Haynes's use of Charles Marsh's and Miroslav Volf's ideas to create a framework of understanding the civil rights movement as theological "spectacles of exclusion and embrace." Haynes, *The Last Segregated Hour*, 15. Haynes uses two sources, Martin Luther King Jr. through Charles Marsh and Miroslav Volf, to establish a way to understand the varied responses to "spectacles" such as the church kneel-ins. The idea of spectacles of "exclusion" and "embrace" helps move our understanding forward to see how theology could be open, but also equally closed, to the "other." By focusing on the "spectacle" we continue to understand white church responses in a singular way. Those moments force responses, and for that reason I think we have a narrowed understanding of "white" churches. For the origin of exclusion and embrace see Miroslav Volf, *Exclusion and Embrace: A Theological Exploration of Identity, Otherness, and Reconciliation* (Nashville, TN: Abingdon Press, 1996).

39. Marsh, *God's Long Summer*, 114–5.

40. Ibid., 31.

41. Joel Alvis (Presbyterians); James F. Findlay Jr., *Church People in the Struggle: The National Council of Churches and the Black Freedom Movement, 1950–1970* (New York: Oxford University Press, 1993).

42. A good example of this willingness to take white ministers on their own terms is S. Jonathan Bass, *Blessed Are the Peacemakers: Martin Luther King Jr., Eight White Religious Leaders, and the "Letter from Birmingham Jail"* (Baton Rouge: Louisiana State University Press, 2001). More recently, Stephen Haynes and Carolyn Dupont have examined white Christian responses to the movement (Haynes, *The Last Segregated Hour* and Dupont, *Praying Mississippi*). In the case of Haynes, the spectacles occurred in the 1960s as an extension of the power of protest to show the hypocrisy of white Christians as they continued to keep black students out of the worship services. In the case of Dupont, white Mississippians continued to construct theological frameworks for segregation. In both cases, however, there is sensitivity to exploring the broad responses of

white Christians. See also Joseph Reiff, *Born of Conviction* (New York: Oxford University Press, 2015).

43. The role of confronting massive resistance fell to a civic group, the Committee for Public Schools, which was made up of religious clerics and lay leaders. "Lists of Members, Richmond Area Committee for Public Schools," Papers of James Rawlings Sydnor, MSS 1 256 a 11–34, Richmond, Virginia Historical Society; Benjamin Muse, *Virginia's Massive Resistance* (Gloucester, MA: Peter Smith, 1969), 55.

Chapter 2

1. For the topic of the NAACP's legal strategy against segregation in the 1940s and 1950s see Mark V. Tushnet, *The NAACP's Legal Strategy against Segregated Education, 1925–1950* (Chapel Hill: University of North Carolina Press, 1987), 115, 135–37.

2. Oliver Hill interview, Richmond, VA, August 23, 1999. (Hereafter "Hill interview.")

3. *Brown et al. v. Board of Education, Topeka et al.*, 347 U.S. 483, 98 L ed 873.

4. Robert Taylor, interview by Douglas E. Thompson, Richmond, VA, March 23, 1997.

5. For a detailed account of the Prince Edward County story, see Robert Smith, *They Closed Their Schools: Prince Edward County, Virginia, 1951–1964* (Chapel Hill: University of North Carolina Press, 1965). In his account, Smith addressed the issue of NAACP involvement in the initial boycott. Smith contends, as many of the African American participants later recounted, that the boycott was student-led and the school desegregation case only occurred after the NAACP realized there was sufficient black community support to sustain a prolonged court battle.

6. Benjamin Muse, *Virginia's Massive Resistance* (Gloucester, MA: Peter Smith, 1969), 6.

7. David L. Chappell, "The Divided Mind of Southern Segregationists," *Georgia Historical Quarterly* XXXII (1998), 45–72. Chappell argues that segregationist politicians could not unite around a single strategy, but unified around two competing arguments for segregation. Kilpatrick was the brainchild of the "constitutional" argument, according to Chappell. David Chappell, *Stone of Hope: Prophetic Religion and the Death of Jim Crow* (Chapel Hill: University of North Carolina Press, 1998), 159–61. In *Stone of Hope*, Chappell expands his earlier argument found in the *Georgia Historical Quarterly* article.

8. It is worth noting that letters to newspaper editors during the 1950s

appear to have been as problematic as comment sections are today. There are varying levels of engagement in the letters and to some extent there are regular contributors who hash out the same points over and over. The difference in this case is the large number of responses. Kilpatrick hit a nerve that shocked both sides of the desegregation debate and revealed most of the arguments that would be used after 1954.

9. "School Segregation: A Decision Lies Ahead," editorial, *Richmond News Leader*, May 7, 1951, 10. For a helpful but limited treatment of Kilpatrick see Ann Elizabeth Burnette, "Tradition and Circumstance: James Jackson Kilpatrick and Massive Resistance," master's thesis, University of Virginia, 1987. For a remarkable treatment of southern "liberal" editors, including Virginius Dabney of the *Richmond Times-Dispatch*, and the issue of race relations, see John T. Kneebone, *Southern Liberal Journalists and the Issue of Race, 1920–1944* (Chapel Hill: University of North Carolina Press, 1985).

10. Jane Daley, *Before Jim Crow: The Politics of Race in Postemancipation Virginia* (Chapel Hill, NC: University of North Carolina Press, 2000), chap. 3. On two occasions, the *Richmond News Leader* posted on its editorial page the number of illegitimate births by race in Virginia noting that black people had a higher rate of illegitimate births, which Kilpatrick apparently thought meant black people were more sexually active than white people. The totals, however, revealed little more than black births and white births without a married spouse present, nor did it take into account rape as a factor. "Changing Racial Pattern in Richmond," editorial, *Richmond News Leader*, February 16, 1955, 12; "It Merits Discussion," editorial, March 22, 1957, 12.

11. Prince Edward County carried on its campaign of resistance until 1963.

12. While other locales closed or threatened to close individual schools, Prince Edward shut its entire system down.

13. "School Segregation," *Richmond News Leader*, May 7, 1951, 10.

14. Kilpatrick's supporters became more numerous by 1955, particularly after his articulation of a "higher plane (States' Rights)" argument for continued segregation.

15. "'Grim Path' Is Held Legal Way to Relief," *Richmond News Leader* Forum, *Richmond News Leader*, May 9, 1951, 10.

16. "Let's Soothe Tempers, and Not Ignite Them," *Richmond News Leader* Forum, *Richmond News Leader*, May 12, 1951, 3.

17. "Racial Separation Held 'Conscienceless,'" *Richmond News Leader* Forum, *Richmond News Leader*, May 14, 1951, 10.

18. For a discussion of the realignment of denominational involvement in politics since World War II, see Robert Wuthnow, *The Restructuring*

of American Religion: Society and Faith since World War II (Princeton, NJ: Princeton University Press, 1988), 148, 315. For works on religion and the "public square," see Michael J. Perry, *Religion in Politics: Constitutional and Moral Perspectives* (New York: Oxford University Press, 1997); Martin E. Marty and Jonathan Moore, *Politics, Religion, and the Common Good: Advancing a Distinctly American Conversation about Religion's Role in Our Shared Life* (San Francisco: Jossey-Bass, 2000); Stephen L. Carter, *God's Name in Vain: The Wrongs and Rights of Religion in Politics* (New York: Basic Books, 2000).

19. *Plessy v. Ferguson*, (1896) 163 U.S. 537.

20. C. Vann Woodward, *The Strange Career of Jim Crow*, 2nd rev. ed. (1955; New York: Oxford University Press, 1966), 71.

21. Leon Friedman, ed., *Argument: The Oral Argument before the Supreme Court in Brown v. Board of Education of Topeka, 1952–55* (New York: Chelsea House, 1969).

22. *Brown et al. v. Board of Education, Topeka et al.*, 98 L ed 873.

23. Some forty-plus years after *Brown* Oliver Hill passionately summed up life in the Jim Crow South: "Segregation didn't just make you feel segregated it made you feel inferior." Oliver Hill, interview by Douglas E. Thompson, Richmond, VA, August 23, 1999.

24. *Brown et al. v. Board of Education, Topeka et al.*, 98 L ed 873, 877.

25. *Brown et al. v. Board of Education, Topeka et al.*, 98 L ed 873, 879–80.

26. *Brown et al. v. Board of Education, Topeka et al.*, 98 L ed 873, 881. For the sources of the court's opinion on the psychological and sociological effects of segregation see note 11 on page 881. The sources included Kenneth Clark's psychological work and Gunnar Myrdal's sociological study, as well as E. Franklin Frazier's historical work on black communities.

27. The only *amicus curiae* briefs filed with the court for any part of the *Brown* case came from the American Jewish Congress, American Civil Liberties Union, American Federation of Teachers, Congress of Industrial Organizations, American Veterans Committee, and Japanese American Citizens League. *Brown et al. v. Board of Education, Topeka et al.*, 347 U.S. 483,485–486, 98 L ed 873, 876; *Brown et al. v. Board of Education, Topeka et al.*, 349 U.S. 294, 99 L ed 1083, 1102, 1103, 1104.

28. Muse, *Virginia's Massive Resistance*, 4.

29. Ernest T. Thompson, *Presbyterians in the South: 1890–1972* (Richmond, VA: John Knox Press, 1973), 539.

30. Thompson, *Presbyterians*, 538–40.

31. John H. Marion, "Let's Face the Basic Issue," *Presbyterian Outlook*, January 15, 1950, 5–6; quoted in Thompson, *Presbyterians*, 534.

32. Thompson, *Presbyterians*, 539.

33. "The Church and Segregation," *Presbyterian Outlook*, May 3, 1954, 1, 5–8; "Segregation End Plea to Be Made," *Richmond News Leader*, May 13, 1954, 18.

34. Thompson, *Presbyterians*, 539.

35. For Baptists, see John Lee Eighmy, *Churches in Cultural Captivity: A History of the Social Attitudes of Southern Baptists* (Knoxville: University of Tennessee Press, 1973), 189–90; also see *Baptist Herald*, June 1954, 4–5. For Methodists, see the resolution found in their *Discipline* (1956).

36. Muse, *Virginia's Massive Resistance*, 5.

37. "The Decision," editorial, *Richmond News Leader*, May 18, 1954, 10.

38. Ibid.

39. Ibid.

40. Letter to Dr. Joe Lee Frank Jr., Ahoskie, NC, January 2, 1956. *Kilpatrick Papers*. Kilpatrick made the same comment to the governor of North Carolina, Luther Hodges, Letter to The Honorable Luther Hodges, Governor of North Carolina, December 21, 1955.

41. "No Bog of Generalities," *Presbyterian Outlook*, May 17, 1954, 8.

42. Ibid.

43. "Church and Segregation," *Presbyterian Outlook*, May 31, 1954, 8.

44. "Bishop Asks Cooperation in Helping Give Catholic Training for Colored," *Catholic Virginian*, May 14, 1954, 1. The *Richmond News Leader* also reported the address. See "Unsegregated Schools Seen for Catholics," *Richmond News Leader*, May 13, 1954, 1, 18. As Ireton had pointed out, Catholic doctrine required black Catholic parents to provide their children with a Catholic education. These parents, like their white counterparts, affirmed their obligation by sending some several hundred students to the Van de Vyrer School. This school, which served the needs of black elementary and middle-school students well into the mid-1960s, had closed its doors to high-school students in 1950.

45. "A Moral, Religious Problem," *Catholic Virginian*, May 21, 1954, 8.

46. For the Catholic Church's response to African American Catholics, see Stephen J. Ochs, *Desegregating the Altar: The Josephites and the Struggle for Black Priests, 1871–1960* (Baton Rouge: Louisiana State University Press, 1990), 1, 2, 8.

47. For the Archdiocese of Richmond's position on African Americans, see Gerald P. Fogarty, *Commonwealth Catholicism: A History of the Catholic Church in Virginia* (Notre Dame, IN: University of Notre Dame Press, 2001).

48. Every year for four years prior to the closing of Van de Vyrer High School there was no mention in the *Catholic Virginian* of commencement exercises at the school, while the other Catholic high schools—all white—received coverage of their closing ceremonies and honored seniors.

49. "Integration in Catholic Schools Set," *Richmond News Leader*, July 15, 1954, 1, 3; "Freshmen Include 11 Colored Pupils," *Catholic Virginian*, September 10, 1954, 1.

50. Christopher Silver and John V. Moeser, *The Separate City: Black Communities in the Urban South, 1940–1968* (Lexington: University Press of Kentucky, 1995), 24.

51. Aubrey Brown Jr., "Aubrey Brown Remembers Race Relations," audiocassette recording, Ginter Park Presbyterian Church, Richmond, VA, May 11, 1997. Brown noted that clause six in the real estate contract read, "No one other than Caucasians."

52. "Editorial," *Baptist Herald*, May 1954, 4.

53. Ibid.

54. Allix B. James, interview by Douglas E. Thompson, Richmond, VA, August 3, 1999; Robert Taylor interview, March 23, 1997.

55. "Editorial," *Baptist Herald*, May 1954, 4–5.

56. Mary L. Dudziak points out that by the mid-1950s Cold War politics affected civil rights history. In this case, Alley acknowledged the liability segregation played in the US's attempt to stop Soviet advances. Mary L. Dudziak, *Cold War Civil Rights: Race and the Image of American Democracy* (Princeton, NJ: Princeton University Press, 2000).

57. "End of Segregation," *Religious Herald*, May 27, 1954, 10.

58. Ibid., 11.

59. "While the World Watches," *Religious Herald*, October 14, 1954, 10–11.

60. Jack H. Manley, "The Next Step in Racial Adjustment," *Religious Herald*, July 1, 1954, 4, 5, 24; John G. Clark, "A Sermon on Segregation and the Christian Conscience," *Religious Herald*, November 11, 1954, 4–5; "Report of the Christian Life Commission to the Baptist General Association of Virginia," *Religious Herald*, December 2, 1954, 4–5, 14, 16.

61. "Unsegregated Public Schools," editorial, *Virginia Methodist Advocate*, May 27, 1954, 10.

62. Ibid.

63. Karen E. Fields, trans., "Translator's Introduction: Religion As An Eminently Social Thing," in *The Elementary Forms of Religious Life* (New York: Free Press, 1995), xxv; Charles H. Lippy, "Popular Religiosity in Central Appalachia," in *Christianity in Appalachia: Profiles in Regional Pluralism*, ed. Bill J. Leonard (Knoxville: University of Tennessee Press, 1999), 46. While Lippy's adherents in central Appalachia may be

more economically disenfranchised than Reamey's readers, his observation is helpful with regard to religion's power to construct reality in people's lives. Writing about the perception of believers as "otherworldly," Lippy asserted, "To take this stance is to miss the way in which the strong conviction of a heavenly afterlife serves to give meaning to the present. Simply put, the heavenly sphere becomes the plane of authentic existence; present reality pales in comparison. Indeed, even the constant struggles of everyday existence here and now take on fresh meaning when viewed from the perspective of eternity."

64. In an attempt to maintain gender neutrality and inclusivity in cases where the gender is indeterminate, I have alternated between using female and male singular pronouns ("she/her" and "he/him"), generally beginning with a female pronoun. For more on Reamey, see Editorial Note to "Objects to Lawrence Editorial," Advocate Mail Box, *Virginia Methodist Advocate*, September 11, 1958, 9.

65. Robert Taylor noted that Ransome disliked the more aggressive actions of the student movement for civil rights. Taylor interview, March 23, 1997.

Chapter 3

1. Benjamin Muse, *Virginia's Massive Resistance* (Gloucester, MA: Peter Smith, 1969), 5; Numan V. Bartley, *The Rise of Massive Resistance: Race and Politics in the South during the 1950's* (Baton Rouge: Louisiana State University Press, 1999), 67.

2. Muse, *Virginia's Massive Resistance*, 7, 8. Benjamin Muse was both a participant observer of the events and one of the first chroniclers of the desegregation battles in Virginia.

3. "Stanley, 2 Ex-Governors Exchange Views on Ruling," *Richmond News Leader*, May 19, 1954, 5.

4. Bartley, *Rise of Massive Resistance*, chap. 5. Bartley argued that border states and Deep South states responded differently to *Brown*. Virginia's response became a model for upper-South states. The initial reaction, however, was moderate and suggested, except for Senator Byrd, that Virginia politicians at least understood *Brown*, and by extension desegregation of public schools, as constitutional.

5. James P. Westberry, "Georgia to Vote on School Issue," *Christian Century*, May 19, 1954, 616.

6. "Pastors Favor Public Schools," *Christian Index*, March 18, 1954, 5.

7. *Christian Index*.

8. *Richmond News Leader*, June 10, 1954, 12; *Afro-American* (Richmond), June 19, 1954, 1–2.

9. *Afro-American* (Richmond), June 19, 1954, 2.

10. Muse, *Virginia's Massive Resistance*, 7.

11. Robbins L. Gates, *The Making of Massive Resistance: Virginia's Politics of Public School Desegregation, 1954–1956* (Chapel Hill: University of North Carolina Press, 1964), 30, 34.

12. Bartley, *Rise of Massive Resistance*, 80.

13. As an example, John Hurt, editor of the *Christian Index*, a Georgia Baptist publication, editorialized on the Gainesville statement but emphasized the importance of caution in moving forward. "Time for Calm," editorial, *Christian Index*, March 18, 1954, 6.

14. Muse, *Virginia's Massive Resistance*, 15.

15. Gates, *Making of Massive Resistance*, 63–72.

16. "Transcendent Issue, II," editorial, *Richmond News Leader*, November 21, 1955, 10; the *Richmond News Leader* republished the series in pamphlet form in December for distribution.

17. Gates, *Making of Massive Resistance*, 104–8. Gates contended that William Old, an attorney from Chesterfield County, "rediscovered" interposition and Kilpatrick "offered it for public sale," 104.

18. Letter to The Honorable Luther Hodges, Governor of North Carolina, December 21, 1955; Letter to Dr. Joe Lee Frank Jr., January 2, 1956, Papers of James Jackson Kilpatrick, University of Virginia, Alderman Library, Charlottesville, VA, MSS 6626-b (Box 61). For a closer examination of Kilpatrick's "fundamental principles" argument, see Ann Elizabeth Burnette, "Tradition and Circumstance: James Jackson Kilpatrick and Massive Resistance," master's thesis, University of Virginia, August 1987. Burnette correctly located Kilpatrick's argument in the context of social unrest and racial tensions of the 1950s and 1960s rather than a universal principle of individual rights. For his personal views on race, see Kilpatrick to Mrs. Claiborne and Select Members of the 20th Precinct Society, July 6, 1956, "Personal File," Box 62, Papers of James Jackson Kilpatrick, University of Virginia, Alderman Library, Charlottesville, VA, MSS 6626-b. "You will recall that the sense of our [neighborhood improvement] meeting was, first, that decisive action should be taken, to the best of our ability, to preserve the character of our neighborhood in the face of a threatened property sale that would disastrously affect our property values." He was referring to the sale of a home in the neighborhood by a black realtor to a black client. The association purchased the property and averted the perceived crisis.

19. "The Right of Interposition," editorial, *Richmond News Leader*, November 22, 1955, 10.

20. Letter to Mr. Harry F. Byrd, Winchester, VA, December 19, 1955, Kilpatrick Papers, Box 61.

21. Muse, *Virginia's Massive Resistance*, 19–23.

22. "Group Formed on Human Relations," *Richmond Times-Dispatch*, February 23, 1953, 1–2; "New Human Relations Group Set to Discuss Desegregation," *Richmond News Leader*, February 23, 1953, 4; "By-laws of the Virginia Council on Human Relations," Papers of the VCHR, 9606, File 1958–1961, "Executive Committee—Minutes, Etc.," Alderman Library, University of Virginia, Charlottesville, VA.

23. "Human Relations," *Richmond Times-Dispatch*, February 23, 1953, 1; "Executive Committee—Minutes, Etc.," VCHR, 9606, File 1958–1961, University of Virginia, Charlottesville, VA.

24. Paul Duke, "Human Relations Group Seeks to Ease Transition For South," *Richmond Times-Dispatch*, November 27, 1955, 6-D. Sent as a clipping from John Marion to Sarah Patton Boyle. Papers of Sarah Patton Boyle, Accession no. 8003-a,-b (Box 4), Special Collections, University of Virginia Library, Charlottesville, VA. The clipping included a handwritten note from Marion: "Patty[,] Good to talk with you this morning. Will write about the article (which says things that should be said) in a day or two. Jack."

25. The Sphinx Club, a Scottish Rite organization, withdrew its invitation for Marion to speak to the group because of his controversial stance on desegregation. *Richmond Times-Dispatch*, December 16, 1955, 3.

26. VCHR Newsletter, vol. 1, no. 8, p. 1; Muse, *Virginia's Massive Resistance*, 36.

27. "Letters to Emerson Smith, VCC, John Marion, VCHR, and Murray Friedman, ADL," January 14, 1955; "Letter to Dumont F. Kenny," January 17, 1955, Box 1, Folder 9, Peter Mellette Papers, 1945–1993, Accession no. 39459, Personal Papers Collection, The Library of Virginia, Richmond, VA.

28. "A Three Session Conference on Human Relations Problems in Education," Box 59, Folder 9, Peter Mellette Papers, 1945–1993, Accession no. 39459, Personal Papers Collection, The Library of Virginia, Richmond, VA.

29. "Proposed School Adjustment Program for Virginia," *Presbyterian Outlook*, November 14, 1955, 1–2.

30. Ibid.

31. Muse, *Virginia's Massive Resistance*, 17; "Baptist Editor Takes Stand Against Constitution Change," *Richmond News Leader*, December 7, 1955, 4; "School Law Change Opposed," *Richmond News Leader*, December 8, 1955, 21; "3rd Faith's Paper Hits Gray Plan," *Richmond News Leader*, December 17, 1955, 1.

32. "For the Sake of Free Public Schools," editorial, *Religious Herald*, December 8, 1955, 10.

33. Gates, *Making of Massive Resistance*, 76; Muse, *Virginia's Massive Resistance*, 86.

34. "The Referendum—Are We Ready to Vote?," editorial, *Virginia Methodist Advocate*, December 8, 1955, 10.

35. Ibid.

36. "Objection 6," editorial, *Richmond News Leader*, December 20, 1955, 12.

37. December 9, 1955, David John Mays, "Diary, 1955," Virginia Historical Society Richmond, VA, MSS 1 M4555e 36.

38. See entry for August 18, 1955, David John Mays, "Diary, 1955."

39. "An Obligation to Vote," editorial, *Catholic Virginian*, December 16, 1955, 8.

40. "Catholic Social Teaching Calls for Vote of 'No' in Referendum, Northern Group Holds," *Catholic Virginian*, December 23, 1955, 2.

41. "Tuition-Grant Plan Threatens Education, Says Women's Council Legislative Chairman," *Catholic Virginian*, December 30, 1955, 1, 16.

42. "The State Referendum," editorial, *Catholic Virginian*, January 6, 1956, 8.

43. "Plight of the Schools," editorial, *Presbyterian Outlook*, December 19, 1955, 8.

44. "The Church in Southern United States," speech delivered before the North American Area Council of the World Presbyterian Alliance, March 17, 1957, Atlantic City, NJ.

45. Aubrey N. Brown Jr., "Standin' in the Need of Prayer," editorial, *Presbyterian Outlook*, November 21, 1955, 8.

46. *Richmond News Leader*, editorial, January 10, 1956; Muse, *Virginia's Massive Resistance*, 21–22; Gates, *Making of Massive Resistance*, 108–16; Bartley, *Rise of Massive Resistance*, 126–30.

47. For the coining of the phrase "massive resistance" see Gates, *Making of Massive Resistance*, 117–18.

48. Gates, *Making of Massive Resistance*, 117; Bartley, *Rise of Massive Resistance*, 111.

49. L. M. Wright Jr., "Group Backs Local Option Integration," *Richmond Times-Dispatch*, August 15, 1956, 1–2; "Human Relations Council Hits Stanley School Stand," *Richmond News Leader*, August 15, 1956, 10; "Local Option Integration is Opposed by Almond," *Richmond Times-Dispatch*, August 16, 1956, 7.

50. Gates, *Making of Massive Resistance*, 168–75. For wilderness metaphor, see Muse, *Virginia's Massive Resistance*, 35.

51. Jeffrey K. Hadden, *The Gathering Storm in the Churches* (Garden City, NY: Doubleday, 1969), 5–6.

52. "Growing Respect Shown for Church Leaders," *Christian Century*, April 28, 1954, 509.

53. Muse, *Virginia's Massive Resistance*, 8.

Chapter 4

1. Numan V. Bartley, *The Rise of Massive Resistance: Race and Politics in the South during the 1950's* (Baton Rouge: Louisiana State University Press, 1999), 293.

2. *Telegraph* (Macon, GA), 1956.

3. "Dog-Bearing Sputnik Circles Globe Every 104 Minutes 1,000 Miles Out," *Constitution* (Atlanta), November 4, 1957, 1.

4. Bartley, *Rise of Massive Resistance*, 296, note 7.

5. "Ministers Provide Guide for Thinking," editorial, *Constitution* (Atlanta), November 4, 1957, 4.

6. "Ministers Rap State's Moves in Race Issue," *Richmond Times-Dispatch*, January 29, 1957, 1, column 2; "Minister's Group Wrong in Saying Bill Curbs Free Speech, Claims Mann," *Richmond Times-Dispatch*, January 30, 1957, 2, column 6.

7. "Clergy's Race Stand Fans Legal Study," *Richmond News Leader*, January 29, 1957, 3, column 3.

8. Bartley, *Rise of Massive Resistance*, 296.

9. "A Statement of Conviction," prepared by the Richmond Ministers' Association, *Richmond Times-Dispatch*, January 29, 1957, 2; also reprinted in *New South*, April 1957, 3–6.

10. "Statement," *Richmond Times-Dispatch*, January 29, 1957, 2.

11. Benjamin Muse, *Virginia's Massive Resistance* (Gloucester, MA: Peter Smith, 1969), 31; Bartley, *Rise of Massive Resistance*, 220–22.

12. "Statement," *Richmond Times-Dispatch*, 2.

13. Ibid.

14. "Clergy's Race Stand Faces Legal Study," *Richmond News Leader*, January 29, 1957, 3.

15. "The Ministers' Statement," editorial, *Richmond News Leader*, January 30, 1957, 10.

16. Lewis F. Powell Oral History Interview, November 5, 1990, Cliff Kuhn and George Butler, interviewers, B-4 (2 tapes), B-8 (transcript), Special Collection, Pullen Library, Georgia State University, Tape 2, Side A, 36–38.

17. Bartley, *Rise of Massive Resistance*, 130.

18. Aubrey Brown Jr., Speech to the Presbyterian Synod WF Conference, November 8, 1963 Camp Hanover, VA.

19. "The Manifesto of the Ministers," editorial, *Richmond Times-Dispatch*, January 31, 1957, 10. For Dabney's transition from a southern liberal to a conservative, see John T. Kneebone, *Southern Liberal Journalists and the Issue of Race, 1920–1944* (Chapel Hill: University of North Carolina Press, 1985), 213.

20. George J. Cleaveland, "Clergyman 'Disassociates' Himself from Document," *Richmond Times-Dispatch*, January 31, 1957, 10.

21. John E. "Parson" Massey, a Baptist preacher from Albemarle, considered himself the "father of the Readjuster movement" and played a significant role in the political intrigue of post–Civil War Virginia, including being elected as lieutenant governor in 1885. Bishop James Cannon Jr. (Methodist) never held political office but was influential in his work with the Anti-Saloon League and the passage of the Prohibition Amendment. Virginius Dabney, *Virginia: The New Dominion* (Garden City, NY: Doubleday, 1971), 383, 395; Virginius Dabney, *Dry Messiah: The Life of Bishop Cannon* (New York: A. A. Knopf, 1949); Sydney E. Ahlstrom, *A Religious History of the American People* (New Haven, CT: Yale University Press, 1972), 902–4.

22. G. MacLaren Brydon, "Ministers' Race Statement Criticized by Clergyman," *Richmond Times-Dispatch*, February 2, 1957, 8.

23. "Charges Clergymen with Creating Tensions," "Says Brief Statement Would Have Sufficed," *Richmond Times-Dispatch*, January 31, 1957, 10; "Says choice is between Segregation, Amalgamation," *Richmond Times-Dispatch*, February 2, 1957, 8; "Ministers Should Stick to the Gospel, He Feels," *Richmond Times-Dispatch*, February 3, 1957, B-2.

24. "'Intelligent, Christian,' He Says of Document," *Richmond Times-Dispatch*, January 31, 1957, 10.

25. The survey was informal because the paper claimed that the RMA had "approximately" 600 members but reached only 180 or 30 percent. See "152 in Survey Favor RMA's Stand on Race: 41 Other Clerics Opposed; 130 Here Noncommittal," (hereafter, Survey) *Richmond Times-Dispatch*, February 4, 1957, 1.

26. "Survey," 1. For a look at how Richmond Catholics differed from their bishop on the racial question, see Gerald Fogarty, *Commonwealth Catholics: A History of the Catholic Church in Virginia* (Notre Dame, IN: University of Notre Dame Press, 2001).

27. "Survey," 4.

28. Bartley, *Rise of Massive Resistance*, 296–97.

29. For Kilpatrick's conversion to Catholicism, see Fogarty, *Commonwealth Catholicism*, 512. For his personal views on race, see Kilpatrick to Mrs. Claiborne and Select Members of the 20th Precinct Society, July 6, 1956, "Personal File," Box 62, Papers of James Jackson Kilpatrick, University of Virginia, Alderman Library, Charlottesville, VA, MSS 6626-b. "You will recall that the sense of our [neighborhood improvement] meeting was, first, that decisive action should be taken, to the best of our ability, to preserve the character of our neighborhood in the face of a threatened property sale that would disastrously affect our property val-

ues." He was referring to the sale of a home in the neighborhood by a black Realtor to a black buyer. The association purchased the property and averted the perceived crisis.

30. Ernest Q. Campbell and Thomas F. Pettigrew, *Christians in Racial Crisis: A Study of Little Rock's Ministry, Including Statements on Desegregation and Race Relations by the Leading Religious Denominations of the United States* (Washington, DC: Public Affairs Press, 1959), 129, 135.

31. James J. Kilpatrick makes an interesting case in point. He publically endorsed the continued segregation of public schools while his bishop (Bishop Ireton, Roman Catholic) sought to desegregate Catholic schools.

32. Bartley, *Rise of Massive Resistance*, 296–97; Bartley cited Myrdal's study about "going on record." See, Gunnar Myrdal, *An American Dilemma: The Negro Problem and Modern Democracy* (New York: Harper & Row, 1962; originally published in 1944), II, 869; Campbell and Pettigrew, *Christians in Crisis*, 11, 20.

33. James H. Hershman Jr., "Massive Resistance Meets its Match: The Emergence of a Pro-Public School Majority," in *The Moderates' Dilemma: Massive Resistance to School Desegregation in Virginia*, ed. Matthew D. Lassiter and Andrew B. Lewis (Charlottesville: University of Virginia Press, 1998), 104; Muse, *Virginia's Massive Resistance*, 107–8.

34. Bartley, *Rise of Massive Resistance*, 296.

35. David L. Chappell, "The Divided Mind of Southern Segregationists," *Georgia Historical Quarterly* LXXXII (1998), 71.

36. Aubrey N. Brown Jr., "Camp Hanover Speech, 1963," Box 20, "Race Relations, 1940s and 1950s," Aubrey Brown Papers, Union Theological Seminary, Richmond, VA. Brown was quoting Robert B. Crawford, first president of the Defenders of State Sovereignty and Individual Liberties, who made the statement during a speech in Charlottesville, VA, in 1955.

Chapter 5

1. Numan V. Bartley, *The Rise of Massive Resistance: Race and Politics in the South during the 1950's* (Baton Rouge: Louisiana State University Press, 1999), 270–71.

2. Benjamin Muse, *Virginia's Massive Resistance* (Gloucester, MA: Peter Smith, 1969), 71–78.

3. Robert A. Pratt, *The Color of Their Skin: Education and Race in Richmond, Virginia 1954–1989* (Charlottesville: University of Virginia Press, 1992).

4. "Officials Confer Here on 3 Integration Bids," *Richmond News Leader*, July 10, 1958, 1; *Richmond News Leader*, July 11, 1958, 1; "A

Little Bigger Cloud," editorial, *Richmond News Leader*, July 11, 1958, 10.

5. "Lists of Members, Richmond Area Committee for Public Schools," Papers of James Rawlings Sydnor, MSS 1 Sy256 a 11–34, Richmond, Virginia Historical Society; Johnston's picture appeared inset with the story "City Ministers Group Blasts State's Moves in Race Issue," *Richmond Times-Dispatch*, January 29, 1957, 2. Johnston was president of the RMA at the release of the statement.

6. "A Round Table Has Debate on Christians' Moral Duty," *Life*, October 1, 1956, 139–162.

7. Ibid., 138–51.

8. Ibid., 139.

9. Ibid., 139–40.

10. Ibid., 140, 43.

11. Ibid., 146, 151.

12. Ibid., 152.

13. Ibid.

14. Peter L. Berger, *Sacred Canopy: Elements of a Sociological Theory of Religion* (New York: Anchor Books, 1990), 22–24. Berger argues that social construction of an ordered universe is inherent in human socialization and an aberration.

15. Rev. R. Bruce Pate, Bridgeton, NC, January 25, 1956; Bishop Garber to Pate, January 30, 1956, Papers of [Paul Neff] Bishop Garber, Box 19, File V A no. 2.09, Randolph Macon University, Ashland, VA.

16. Paul Neff Garber to J. W. Luter, Smithfield, VA, January 6, 1956, Box 19, File V A no. 2.10. See also, Rufus Copeland, Lasker, NC, to Bishop Garber, November 19, 1958, Box 19, File V A no. 1.02; Garber to Copeland, December 3, 1958, Box 19, File V A no. 2.10a; Edmund Price to Garber, Kinston, NC, November 20, 1958; Garber to Price, December 8, 1958.

17. Elmore Brown, *Paul Neff Garber: A Bishop of Destiny* (Richmond, VA: No publisher, 1978), 135–48.

18. George Reamey, "Integration and Moral Standards," editorial, *Virginia Methodist Advocate*, July 10, 1958, 10.

19. "Moral Standards," *Virginia Methodist Advocate*, July 10, 1958, 10; *Richmond News Leader*, June 26, 1958, 10. Kilpatrick published "Integration and Moral Standards" on his editorial page without comment.

20. Aubrey N. Brown Jr., "Race Relations, 1940s and 1950s," Box 20, Aubrey Brown Papers, Union Theological Seminary in Virginia, Richmond, VA; *Richmond News Leader*, February 4, 1960, 1.

21. "Says Negro Race Bears Stigma for Interracial Offspring," *Virginia Methodist Advocate*, July 24, 1958, 6.

22. "Wants Editorial Widely Circulated," "Says Negro Race Bears

Stigma for Interracial Offspring," *Virginia Methodist Advocate*, July 24, 1958, 6; "Should Be Widely Read," "Calibre of Congress at All-Time High," "Not Necessary To Be Integrationist To Be Christian," *Virginia Methodist Advocate*, July 31, 1958, 11.

23. David Lawrence, "The People Speak," editorial reprinted from *US News & World Report* in *Virginia Methodist Advocate*, August 7, 1958, 10; "Objects to Lawrence Editorial," "Disagrees With Hough," *Virginia Methodist Advocate*, September 11, 1958, 8–9.

24. Lawrence, "People Speak," *Virginia Methodist Advocate*, 10.

25. Hough, "Objects," 7.

26. Ibid.

27. "Lawrence," editorial, *Virginia Methodist Advocate*, August 28, 1958, 11, 14.

28. Letter from Edmund Price, November 20, 1958 to Garber. The letter asked Garber his position on the recent College of Bishops' resolution on integration. Garber responded: "I wish we could have a talk for you certainly are not acquainted with my views on the present most difficult problem before all of us. I have never approved any resolutions endorsing the action of the Supreme Court. If you read my statement in the Life Symposium (Cf. *Life* October 1, 1956) of a few years ago, you would know that I stated that it was the right of the parents to decide under what circumstances their children were to be educated. I did not vote for the recent resolution of the Council of Bishops and when a similar resolution was passed several years ago I, with eight other bishops, had our names recorded in the Minutes as opposing the resolution. If you will study my record you will find that perhaps we hold very similar views." Letter from Garber to Edmund Price, December 8, 1958, Garber Papers, Box 19, File V A no. 2.10a.

29. "Disagrees with Hough," *Virginia Methodist Advocate*, 9; "Doing a Disservice," "Objects to Lawrence Editorial," "Shows Inherent Weakness," *Virginia Methodist Advocate*, September 11, 1958, 8–9, 16.

30. Letter from George Reamey to Bishop Paul Garber, July 16, 1958, Garber File V A no. 10.01. In the letter to Garber, Reamey confided that the content of the letter might cause a disruption to the ongoing capital campaign at Ferrum College, then a junior college owned by the conference. He wrote: "You realize of course that if we published his letter it could and probably would have a hurtful effect on the Ferrum million-dollar campaign now under way." Reamey included that he wrote a correspondence to a Ferrum administrator and said that he "mentioned the campaign and told him that if he wants the letter printed the Advocate would 'assume no responsibility whatever for any consequences to the campaign which may ensue.'"

31. "Shows Inherent Weakness," *Virginia Methodist Advocate*, 9, 16.

32. *Doctrines and Discipline of the Methodist Church, 1956* (Richmond, VA: Methodist Publishing House, 1957) 723–24.

33. Segregation via the Central Jurisdiction was done away with in 1968 when the United Methodist Church came into existence from a merger of the Evangelical United Brethren and the Methodists.

34. "Richmond District Ministers Request Printing of Church Law on Race Relations," *Virginia Methodist Advocate*, October 9, 1958, 8–9; *Virginia Methodist Advocate*, June 19, 1958, 3.

35. See Garber, Box 19, File V, A no. 1.02; Garber, Box 19, File V, A no. 2.10a. One document in the Garber files includes handwritten notes on a copy of a six-page proposed resolution from the Southeast and Central Jurisdictions regarding the racial crisis and the use of Methodist buildings for private schools. In the notes, it appeared that Garber contended that the bishops had no right to tell boards of churches what they could and could not do with their property. Garber, undated, Box 19, File V, A no. 18.02.

36. "Why Not A Boys' School at Blackstone?," editorial, *Virginia Methodist Advocate*, October 16, 1958, 10.

37. Andrew E. Murray, *Presbyterians and the Negro—A History* (Philadelphia, PA: Presbyterian Historical Society, 1966), 180–81.

38. Ernest T. Thompson, *Presbyterians in the South*, Vol. 3: 1890–1972 (Richmond, VA: John Knox Press, 1973), 201–2.

39. Thompson, *Presbyterians*, 490.

40. Thompson, *Presbyterians*, 491–92. For Thompson, the southern Presbyterian church remained largely conservative—biblically centered—but was moving away from "the *jure divino*, 'Thus saith the Lord' ecclesiasticism of the earlier period" (490).

41. Ken Goodpasture, a former director of graduate studies at Union Theological Seminary in Virginia, noted that the biggest impression about the importance of racial equality occurred when he attended a biracial gathering coordinated by Elinor Curry, a white woman, at the 17th Street Mission in Richmond's Eastend. Curry held these meetings on Sunday evenings and invited students from Union, Presbyterian School of Christian Education, and Virginia Union University to discuss pressing issues of the day. Goodpasture remembered the event as the first time in his young life that he sat down to talk to a black person with the same educational background as peers. Ken Goodpasture, interview by Douglas E. Thompson, Richmond, VA, August 3, 1999.

42. William N. Todd, "The Atomic Era," in *Virginia Presbyterians in American Life: Hanover Presbytery (1755–1980)*, Patricia Aldridge, ed. (Richmond, VA: Hanover Presbytery, 1982), 235.

43. Goodpasture interview, August 3, 1999.

44. Todd, "Atomic Era," 239.

45. Aubrey Brown III, interview by Douglas E. Thompson, Washington, DC, August 18, 1999.

46. Todd, "Atomic Era," 239–40.

47. Quoted in Thompson, *Presbyterians*, 497.

48. As noted earlier in this book, John Bright authored a much-used text on the history of Israel (*A History of Israel*. 1959. 3rd ed. Philadelphia: Westminster Press, 1981) as well as *Covenant and Promise: The Prophetic Understanding of the Future in Pre-Exilic Israel*. Without Brown's corresponding letter it is unclear which, if either, of these texts Brown referred to.

49. Letter from John Bright to Aubrey N. Brown Jr., February 19, 1957, Aubrey Brown Papers, Box 20, "Race Relations 1940s and 1950s," Morton Library, Union Theological Seminary, Virginia, Richmond, VA.

50. First Richmond, Session Minutes, June 26, 1957, quoted in Todd, "Atomic Era," 241.

51. Minutes of winter and spring meetings of Hanover Presbytery, May 27, 1958, 31.

52. I am indebted to Aubrey Brown III for his affirmation of my "hunch." He knows Thomas Pettigrew and challenged him on his lack of insight on this subject in Pettigrew's Little Rock study. For Presbyterian denominational polity, see Frank S. Mead, *Handbook of Denominations in the United States*, revised by Samuel S. Hill, 9th ed. (Nashville, TN: Abingdon Press, 1990), 203–9.

53. Todd, "Atomic Era," 243.

54. First Richmond, Session Minutes, October 23, 1957, quoted in Todd, "Atomic Era," 242.

55. Todd, "Atomic Era," 243; Minutes, Hanover Presbytery, May 27, 1958, 32.

56. *Richmond Times-Dispatch*, May 28, 1958, 1, 4; *Richmond News Leader*, May 28, 1958, 16; *Presbyterian Outlook*, June 7, 1958, 2. First Richmond, along with Second Richmond, overtured the presbytery again in 1959 regarding Camp Hanover and once again the presbytery affirmed its stand for full integration at the camp.

57. Editorials, *Richmond News Leader*, November 11–12, 1958, 10; Editorial, *Richmond Times-Dispatch*, November 12, 1958, 12; Muse, *Virginia's Massive Resistance*, 94–98; Bartley, *Rise of Massive Resistance*, 320–21; Oliver Hill, interview, August 23, 1999. Oliver Hill's son attended Chandler Middle School—located in Barton Heights—in 1961, and two girls attended John Marshall High School.

Epilogue

1. Constance Baker Motley, *Equal Justice under the Law: An Autobiography* (New York: Farrar, Straus and Giroux, 1998), 130–32. The NAACP's legal strategy had sidestepped this issue on purpose because precedent had been established by the court when it rejected the 1875 Civil Rights Act, which had required open access to private facilities providing public accommodations.

2. "Attack Sitdowners," *Afro-American* (Richmond), February 20, 1960, 1–2; "40 Cheered To Jail," *Afro-American* (Richmond), February 27, 1960, 1–2.

3. "The Sit Downs," editorial, *Richmond News Leader*, February 22, 1960, 8.

4. A picture on the front page of the *Afro-American* (Richmond), March 12, 1960, showed three students identified with the Union Theological Seminary in Richmond over a caption that stated: "Show of Brotherhood."

5. Undated memo in the Papers of Aubrey N. Brown Jr., Virginia Historical Society, Series 1, noted that between 175 and 200 students from both schools participated in discussions about the protest for more than five hours.

6. Papers of Aubrey N. Brown Jr., MSS 1 B8122nFA2, Virginia Historical Society, Series 1, Folder 1.

7. Papers of Aubrey N. Brown, VHS, Series 1, "Sit-ins" Folder.

8. Letter from George Reamey to Aubrey Brown Jr., December 15, 1966, page 3, Papers of Aubrey N. Brown, Series 14, Folders 1–2.

9. Letter from Aubrey Brown Jr. to George Reamey, December 21, 1966, Papers of Aubrey N. Brown, Series 14, Folder 1–2.

BIBLIOGRAPHY

Primary Sources

Boyle, Sarah Patton. Papers. Box. 4. Accession no. 8003-a,-b. Albert and Shirley Smalls Special Collections, University of Virginia Library, Charlottesville.

Brown, Aubrey. Papers. "Race Relations, 1940s and 1950s." Box 20. Special Collections, William Smith Morton Library, Union Theological Seminary, Richmond, VA.

Brown, Aubrey N. Papers. 1944–1995. MSS 1 B8122aFA2. Virginia Historical Society, VA.

Brown et al. v. Board of Education, Topeka et al., 347 U.S. (1954): 483.

Brown et al. v. Board of Education, Topeka et al., 98 L ed (1954): 873.

The Fellowship of Southern Churchmen. Records. No. 3479. Southern Historical Collection, Wilson Library, University of North Carolina at Chapel Hill.

Garber, Bishop (Paul Neff). Papers. Box 19. Randolph Macon University, Ashland, VA.

Kilpatrick, James Jackson. Papers. Box 61. MSS 6626-b. Albert and Shirley Smalls Special Collections, University of Virginia, Charlottesville.

Kuhn, Cliff, and George Butler. B-2 (2 tapes), B-4 (manuscript). 1990. Lewis F. Powell Oral History Interview. Georgia State University, Atlanta.

Marion, John J., Jr. 1943. "Magnificent Obsession: A Sermon Preached at Grace Covenant Presbyterian Church, Richmond, Virginia." General Collection, Virginia Historical Society, VA.

Mays, David John. Papers. Box 36. MSS 1 M4555e. "Diary, 1955." Virginia Historical Society, VA.

Smith, Robert Lee. 1893. *Barton Heights, The Popular Suburb of Richmond.* Albert and Shirley Smalls Special Collections, University of Virginia, Charlottesville.

Sydnor, James Rawlings. Papers. MSS 1 256 a 11–34. Virginia Historical Society, VA.

Virginia State Constitution, Section 31 (1902).

Periodicals

Afro-American (Richmond), 1946, 1954, 1960.

Baptist Herald (Richmond), 1954.

Catholic Virginian (Richmond), 1950, 1951, 1954, 1955, 1956.

Constitution (Atlanta), 1957.

Presbyterian Outlook (Richmond), 1954, 1955, 1958.

Religious Herald (Richmond), 1954, 1955.

Richmond Ministers' Association. "A Statement of Conviction." *Richmond Times-Dispatch*, January 29, 1957, 2.

Richmond News Leader, 1939, 1941, 1949–1951, 1953–1960.

Richmond Times-Dispatch, 1943, 1947, 1949, 1953, 1955–1958, 1960.

Telegraph (Macon, GA), 1956.

Virginia Methodist Advocate (Richmond), 1954, 1955, 1958.

Interviews

Brown, Aubrey, III. Interview by Douglas E. Thompson. Washington, DC, August 18, 1999.

Goodpasture, Ken. Interview by Douglas E. Thompson. Richmond, VA, August 3, 1999.

Hill, Oliver. Interview by Douglas E. Thompson. Richmond, VA, August 23, 1999.

James, Allix B. Interview by Douglas E. Thompson. Richmond, VA, August 3, 1999.

Taylor, Robert. Interview by Douglas E. Thompson. Richmond, VA, March 23, 1997.

Secondary Sources

Ahlstrom, Sydney E. *A Religious History of the American People.* New Haven, CT: Yale University Press, 1972.

Ayers, Edward L. *The Promise of the New South: Life after Reconstruction.* New York: Oxford University Press, 1992.

Bailey, Kenneth K. *Southern White Protestantism in the Twentieth Century.* New York: Harper & Row, 1964.

Bartley, Numan V. *The Rise of Massive Resistance: Race and Politics in the South during the 1950's*. 1969. Baton Rouge: Louisiana State University Press, 1999.

"Barton Heights Neighborhood." *Richmond Magazine*, June 1976.

Bass, S. Jonathan. *Blessed Are the Peacemakers: Martin Luther King Jr., Eight White Religious Leaders, and the "Letter from Birmingham Jail"*. Baton Rouge: Louisiana State University Press, 2001.

Berger, Peter L. *Sacred Canopy: Elements of a Sociological Theory of Religion*. 1969. New York: Anchor Books, 1990.

Berger, Peter L., and Thomas Luckman. *The Social Construction of Reality: A Treatise in the Sociology of Knowledge*. New York: Anchor Books, 1967.

Bright, John. *Covenant and Promise: The Prophetic Understanding of the Future in Pre-Exilic Israel*. Philadelphia, PA: Westminster John Know Press, 1976.

———. *A History of Israel*. 1959. 3rd ed. Philadelphia: Westminster Press, 1981.

Brown, Elmore. *Paul Neff Garber: A Bishop of Destiny*. Richmond, VA: No Publisher, 1978.

Buni, Andrew. *The Negro in Virginia Politics 1902–1965*. Charlottesville: University of Virginia Press, 1967.

Burnette, Ann Elizabeth. "Tradition and Circumstance: James Jackson Kilpatrick and Massive Resistance." Master's thesis, University of Virginia, 1987.

Campbell, Ernest Q., and Thomas F. Pettigrew. *Christians in Racial Crisis: A Study of Little Rock's Ministry, Including Statements on Desegregation and Race Relations by the Leading Religious Denominations of the United States*. Washington, DC: Public Affairs Press, 1959.

Campbell. Will D. *Race and the Renewal of the Church*. Philadelphia: Westminster Press, 1962.

Carter, Stephen L. *God's Name in Vain: The Wrongs and Rights of Religion in Politics*. New York: Basic Books, 2000.

Chappell, David L. "The Divided Mind of Southern Segregationists." *Georgia Historical Quarterly* XXXII (1998): 45–72.

———. *Inside Agitators: White Southerners and the Civil Rights Movement*. Baltimore, MD: Johns Hopkins University Press, 1996.

———. *A Stone of Hope: Prophetic Religion and the Death of Jim Crow*. Chapel Hill: University of North Carolina Press, 2005.

Chesson, Michael B. *Richmond after the War: 1865–1890*. Richmond: Virginia State Library, 1981.

Curry, Henry Lee, III. "The Confederate Careers of James Armstrong Duncan, Moses Drury Hoge, and Charles Frederic Ernest Minnigerode." PhD diss., Emory University, Atlanta, GA, 1971.

Dabney, Virginius. *Across the Years: Memories of a Virginian*. Garden City, NY: Doubleday, 1978.

———. *Dry Messiah: The Life of Bishop Cannon*. New York: A. A. Knopf, 1949.

———. *Richmond: The Story of a City*, rev. and expanded. 1990. Charlottesville: University of Virginia Press, 1976.

———. *Virginia: The New Dominion*. Garden City, NY: Doubleday, 1971.

Dailey, Jane. *Before Jim Crow: The Politics of Race in Postemancipation Virginia*. Chapel Hill: University of North Carolina Press, 2000.

Daniel, Pete. *Lost Revolutions: The South in the 1950s*. Chapel Hill: University of North Carolina Press, 2000.

Douglas, Lloyd. *Magnificent Obsession*. New York: Willett, Clark & Colby, 1929.

Dudziak, Mary L. *Cold War Civil Rights: Race and the Image of American Democracy*. Princeton, NJ: Princeton University Press, 2000.

Dunbar, Anthony P. *Against the Grain: Southern Radicals and Prophets, 1929–1959*. Charlottesville: University of Virginia Press, 1981.

———. "Fellowship of Southern Churchmen." In *Encyclopedia of Religion in the South*, edited by Samuel S. Hill Jr., 316–17. Macon, GA: Mercer University Press, 1984.

Dupont, Carolyn. *Mississippi Praying: Southern White Evangelicals and the Civil Rights Movement, 1945–1975*. New York: New York University Press, 2013.

Durkheim, Emile. *The Elementary Forms of Religious Life*. 1912. Translated by Karen E. Fields. New York: Free Press, 1995.

Egerton, John. *Speak Now against the Day: The Generation before the Civil Rights Movement in the South*. Chapel Hill: University of North Carolina Press, 1995.

Eighmy, John Lee. *Churches in Cultural Captivity: A History of the Social Attitudes of Southern Baptists*. Knoxville: University of Tennessee Press, 1973.

Federal Workers of the Writers' Program of Virginia. *The Negro in Virginia*. New York: Hastings House, 1940.

Fields, Karen E. "Translator's Introduction." In *The Elementary Forms of Religious Life*, x–lxxiii. New York: Free Press, 1995.

Findlay Jr., James F. *Church People in the Struggle: The National Council of Churches and the Black Freedom Movement, 1950–1970*. New York: Oxford University Press, 1993.

Fogarty, Gerald P. *Commonwealth Catholicism: A History of the Catholic Church in Virginia*. Notre Dame, IN: University of Notre Dame Press, 2001.

Friedman, Leon, ed. *Argument: The Oral Argument before the Supreme Court in Brown v. Board of Education of Topeka, 1952–55*. New York: Chelsea House, 1969.

Gates, Robbins L. *The Making of Massive Resistance: Virginia's Politics of Public School Desegregation, 1954–1956*. Chapel Hill: University of North Carolina Press, 1964.

Geertz, Clifford. "Religion as a Cultural System." In *The Religious Situation*, edited by Donald R. Culter, 639–88. Boston, MA: Beacon Press, 1968.

Goldfield, David R. *Black, White, and Southern: Race Relations and Southern Culture 1940 to the Present*. Baton Rouge: Louisiana State University Press, 1990.

Guild, June Purcell. *Black Laws of Virginia: A Summary of the Legislative Acts of Virginia Concerning Negroes from Earliest Times to the Present*. 1936. 4th ed. Lovettesville, VA: Willow Bend Books, 1996.

Hadden, Jeffery K. *The Gathering Storm in the Churches*. Garden City, NY: Doubleday, 1969.

Hale, Grace Elizabeth. *Making Whiteness: The Culture of Segregation in the South, 1890–1940*. New York: Pantheon Books, 1998.

Harvey, Paul. *Freedom's Coming: Religious Culture and the Shaping of the South from the Civil War though the Civil Rights Era*. Chapel Hill: University or North Carolina Press, 2005.

Haynes, Stephen R. *The Last Segregated Hour: The Memphis Kneel-Ins and the Campaign for Southern Church Desegregation*. New York: Oxford University Press, 2012.

Hershman, James H., Jr. "Massive Resistance Meets Its Match: The Emergence of a Pro-Public School Majority." In *The Moderates' Dilemma: Massive Resistance to School Desegregation in Virginia*, edited by Matthew D. Lassiter and Andrew B. Lewis, 104–33. Charlottesville: University of Virginia Press, 1998.

Heschel, Abraham J. *The Prophets: An Introduction*. 2 vols. New York: Harper & Row, 1969.

Hill, Samuel, S. *Southern Churches in Crisis*. New York: Henry Holt, 1966.

Hoehling, A. A., and Mary Hoehling. *The Day Richmond Died*. New York: Madison Books, 1981.

Johnson, Nessa Theresa Baskerville. *A Special Pilgrimage: A History of Black Catholics in Richmond*. Richmond, VA: Whittet and Shepperson, 1978.

Key, V. O., Jr., and Alexander Heard. *Southern Politics in State and Nation*. New York: A. A. Knopf, 1949.

Kimball, Gregg. *American City, Southern Place: A Cultural History of Antebellum Richmond*. Athens: University of Georgia Press, 2000.

Kneebone, John T. *Southern Liberal Journalists and the Issue of Race, 1920–1944*. Chapel Hill: University of North Carolina Press, 1985.

Lippy, Charles H. "Popular Religiosity in Central Appalachia." In *Christianity in Appalachia: Profiles in Regional Pluralism*, edited by Bill J. Leonard, 40–51. Knoxville: University of Tennessee Press, 1999.

Marion, John J., Jr. "Courtesy Across the Color Line." *Christian Century* LVII, no. 20 (May 15, 1940), 639.

———. "Farewell, My Lovely Magnolias." *Yale Review* XXXV, no. 3 (March 1946).

Marsh, Charles. *God's Long Summer: Stories of Faith and Civil Rights*. Princeton, NJ: Princeton University Press, 1997.

Marty, Martin E., and Jonathan Moore. *Politics, Religion, and the Common Good: Advancing a Distinctly American Conversation about Religion's Role in Our Shared Life*. San Francisco: Jossey-Bass, 2000.

Mead, Frank S. *Handbook of Denominations in the United States*, revised by Samuel S. Hill, 9th ed. Nashville, TN: Abingdon Press, 1990.

Methodist Episcopal Church, South. *Doctrines and Discipline of the Methodist Church*, 1956. Richmond, VA: Methodist Publishing House, 1957.

Mobley, Constance Baker. *Equal Justice under the Law: An Autobiography*. New York: Farrar, Straus and Giroux, 1998.

Moger, Allen. *Virginia: Bourbonism to Byrd 1870–1925*. Charlottesville: University of Virginia Press, 1968.

Murray, Andrew E. *Presbyterians and the Negro—A History*. Philadelphia, PA: Presbyterian Historical Society, 1966.

Muse, Benjamin. *Virginia's Massive Resistance*. Gloucester, MA: Peter Smith, 1969.

Myrdal, Gunnar. *An American Dilemma: The Negro Problem and Modern Democracy*. New York: Harper & Row, 1944.

Ochs, Stephen J. *Desegregating the Altar: The Josephites and the Struggle for Black Priests, 1871–1960*. Baton Rouge: Louisiana State University Press, 1990.

O'Connor, Flannery. "Revelation" In *Everything That Rises Must Converge*, 191–218. New York: Farrar, Straus and Giroux, 1998.

Patrick, Rembert W. *The Fall of Richmond*. Baton Rouge: Louisiana State University Press, 1960.

Perry, Michael J. *Religion in Politics: Constitutional and Moral Perspectives*. New York: Oxford University Press, 1997.

Peterson, Richard A., and N. J. Demerath III. "Introduction." In Liston Pope, *Millhands and Preachers: A Study of Gastonia*, xvii–xlix. New Haven, CT and London: Yale University Press, 1942.

Pratt, Robert A. *The Color of Their Skin: Education and Race in Rich-*

mond, Virginia 1954–1989. Charlottesville: University of Virginia Press, 1992.

Reiff, Joseph. *Born of Conviction: White Methodists and Mississippi's Closed Society*. New York: Oxford University Press, 2015.

"A Round Table Has Debate on Christians' Moral Duty." *Life*, October 1, 1956, 139–62.

Russell, John H. *The Free Negro in Virginia 1619–1865*. 1913. New York: Dover, 1969.

Ryan, David D. *Four Days in 1865: The Fall of Richmond*. Richmond, VA: Cadmus Communications Corporation, 1993.

Schweiger, Beth Barton. *The Gospel Working Up: Progress and the Pulpit in Nineteenth-Century Virginia*. New York: Oxford University Press, 2000.

Shattuck, Gardiner H., Jr. *Episcopalians & Race: Civil War to Civil Rights*. Lexington: University Press of Kentucky, 2000.

Shepherd, Samuel C., Jr. *Avenues of Faith: Shaping the Urban Religious Culture of Richmond, Virginia, 1900–1929*. Tuscaloosa: University of Alabama Press, 2001.

Silver, Christopher. *Twentieth-Century Richmond: Planning, Politics, and Race*. Knoxville: University of Tennessee Press, 1984.

Silver, Christopher, and John V. Moeser. *The Separate City: Black Communities in the Urban South, 1940–1968*. Lexington: University Press of Kentucky, 1995.

Smith, Robert. *They Closed Their Schools: Prince Edward County, Virginia, 1951–1964*. Chapel Hill: University of North Carolina Press, 1965.

Steinhorn, Leonard, and Barbara Diggs-Brown. *By the Color of Our Skin: The Illusions of Integration and the Reality of Race*. New York: A Dutton Book, 1999.

Taylor, Michael Eric. "The African-American Community of Richmond, Virginia: 1950–1956." Master's thesis, University of Richmond, 1994.

Thompson, Ernest T. "From Civil War to World War (1861–1914)." In *Virginia Presbyterians in American Life: Hanover Presbytery (1755–1980)*, edited by Patricia Aldridge, 103–56. Richmond, VA: Hanover Presbytery, 1982.

———. *Presbyterians in the South: 1890–1972*. 3 vols. Richmond, VA: John Knox Press, 1973.

Todd, William Newton. "The Atomic Era." In *Virginia Presbyterians in American Life: Hanover Presbytery (1755–1980)*, edited by Patricia Aldridge. Richmond, VA: Hanover Presbytery, 1982.

Trevvett, W. Stuart. *The Methodist of Barton Heights in Richmond, Virginia 1892–1978*. Richmond, VA: Whittet and Shepperson, 1981.

Troeltsch, Enst. *The Social Teaching of the Christian Churches.* 1911. Translated by Olive Wyon. New York: Harper & Brothers, 1960.

Tushnet, Mark V. *The NAACP's Legal Strategy against Segregated Education, 1925–1950.* Chapel Hill: University of North Carolina Press, 1987.

Volf, Miroslav. *Exclusion and Embrace: A Theological Exploration of Identity, Otherness, and Reconciliation.* Nashville, TN: Abingdon Press, 1996.

White, Blanche Sydnor. *First Baptist Church Richmond, 1780–1955.* Richmond, VA: Whittet and Shepperson, 1955.

Woodward, C. Vann. *Origins of the New South 1877–1913.* 1951. Baton Rouge: Louisiana State University Press, 1971.

———. *The Strange Career of Jim Crow.* 2nd rev. ed. New York: Oxford University Press, 1966.

Wuthnow, Robert. *The Restructuring of American Religion: Society and Faith since World War II.* Princeton, NJ: Princeton University Press, 1988.

Wynes, Charles E. *Race Relations in Virginia 1870–1902.* Charlottesville: University of Virginia Press, 1961.

INDEX